Lefevre James Cranstone

His Life and Art

Lefevre James Cranstone

His Life and Art

By Donald L. Smith

Brandylane Publishers, Inc.

Richmond, Virginia

Printed in China.

Brandylane Publishers, Inc.
Richmond, Virginia
800 553 6922
Email: *brandy@crosslink.net*
www.brandylanepublishers.com

Cover Image: Lefevre James Cranstone, *Slave Auction, Virginia,* 1863, oil on fabric,
13 x 21 in. Courtesy, Virginia Historical Society, Richmond, Virginia.
Cover Design by Thomas Trenz

ISBN 1-883911-60-5   160308- 1001

Library of Congress Control Number - 2004090445

This book is dedicated to my wife, Jan, for the love, friendship,
encouragement and insightful suggestions she has provided,
not only while researching and writing this book,
but also during our lives together.

CONTENTS

List of Illustrations   viii

Foreword   xvii

Acknowledgments   xix

Introduction   xxi

1. Journey to America   1

2. Places Visited, 1859-1860   6

3. On Slavery   85

4. More Watercolor Paintings   89

5. His Life and Career in England   98

6. Australia, 1883-1893   115

Epilogue   130

Letter to Hemel Hempstead Gazette, dated December 29, 1860   131

Exhibitions of Cranstone's Paintings in America, England, and Australia   136

Auctions of Cranstone's Paintings in America, England, and Australia   139

Notes   142

Bibliography   147

Index   151

ILLUSTRATIONS

Chapter 1

1.1   Lefevre James Cranstone, c. 1859, photograph, Palladium-Item, April 9, 1951. Courtesy, Palladium-Item, Richmond, Indiana.

1.2   *Steamer Kangaroo*, built 1853, photograph. Courtesy, Mariners' Museum, Newport News, VA.

1.3   Frances, William Henry, Eliza, Alfred and Lefevre James Cranstone, Hemel Hempstead, England, 1860, photograph, D/ECe/F41. Courtesy, Hertfordshire Archives & Local Studies, Hertford, England.

Chapter 2
Unless otherwise noted, images printed in Chapter 2 were provided courtesy of The Lilly Library, Indiana University, Bloomington, Indiana.

2.1   Lefevre James Cranstone, *The Kangaroo Sept. 2nd,* 1859, 4½ x 7½ in.

2.2   Lefevre James Cranstone, *Deck of the Kangaroo,* 1859, 4½ x 7½ in.

2.3   Lefevre James Cranstone, *Market Place, Halifax,* 1859, 4½ x 7½ in.

2.4   Lefevre James Cranstone, *Halifax, N.S.,* 1859, 4½ x 7½ in.

2.5   Lefevre James Cranstone, *Dartmouth, Nova Scotia, September 16th 1859,* 1859, 4½ x 7½ in.

2.6   Lefevre James Cranstone, *The Kangaroo Landing Passengers, New York, September 19th,* 1859, 4½ x 7½ in.

2.7   Lefevre James Cranstone, *McCulloch's Leap, Wheeling, Va. September 1859,* 1859, 4½ x 7½ in.

2.8   Lefevre James Cranstone, *Tunnel, Hempfield & Wheeling Line, Va. October 1859,* 1859, 4½ x 7½ in.

2.9   Lefevre James Cranstone, *Railway Bridge near Wheeling, Va. October 2nd 1859,* 1859, 4½ x 7½ in.

2.10   Lefevre James Cranstone, *Methodist Church & School House, Fulton, Va.,* 1859, 4½ x 7½ in.

2.11   Lefevre James Cranstone, *Nr. Wheeling, Virginia,* 1859, 4½ x 7½ in.

2.12   Lefevre James Cranstone, *Nr. Wheeling, Virginia,* 1859, 4½ x 7½ in.

2.13   Lefevre James Cranstone, *Near Wheeling, Virginia*, 1859, 4½ x 7½ in.

2.14   Lefevre James Cranstone, *Ohio River, Nr. Wheeling*, 1859, 4½ x 7½ in.

2.15   Lefevre James Cranstone, *The Ohio River*, 1859, 4½ x 7½ in.

2.16   Lefevre James Cranstone, *McCulloch's Leap, Wheeling, Virginia*, 1859, 4½ x 7½ in.

2.17   Lefevre James Cranstone, *Hempfield Railway, Nr. Wheeling, Virginia* 1859,
        4½ x 7½ in.

2.18   Lefevre James Cranstone, *Nr. Bridgeport, Ohio*, 1859, 4½ x 7½ in.

2.19   Lefevre James Cranstone, *Mills, near Wheeling, Va. October 1859*, 1859, 4½ x 7½ in.

2.20   Lefevre James Cranstone, *Nr. Wheeling, Va. October 1859*, 1859, 4½ x 7½ in.

2.21   Lefevre James Cranstone, *Poor House, Wheeling October 1859*, 1859, 4½ x 7½ in.

2.22   Lefevre James Cranstone, *Wheeling, from Ohio November 1859*, 1859, 4½ x 7½ in.

2.23   Lefevre James Cranstone, *Ohio, November 1859*, 1859, 4½ x 7½ in.

2.24   Lefevre James Cranstone, *Nr. Ohio, November 1859*, 1859, 4½ x 7½ in.

2.25   Lefevre James Cranstone, *Ohio, November 1859*, 1859, 4½ x 7½ in.

2.26   Lefevre James Cranstone, *At the Wharf, Wheeling, Virginia*, 1859, 4½ x 7½ in.

2.27   Lefevre James Cranstone, *Suspension Bridge, Ohio River, Wheeling, Virginia*, 1859,
        4½ x 7½ in.

2.28   Lefevre James Cranstone, *Parkersburg, Va. November 1859*, 1859, 4½ x 7½ in.

2.29   Lefevre James Cranstone, *Parkersburg, Virginia November 1859*, 1859, 4½ x 7½ in.

2.30   Frederick, Ellen and Albert Lefevre, Richmond, Indiana, c. 1860, photograph,
        D/ECe/F138. Courtesy, Hertfordshire Archives & Local Studies, Hertfordshire,
        England.

2.31   Lefevre James Cranstone, *Richmond, Indiana*, 1859, 4½ x 7½ in.

2.32   Lefevre James Cranstone, *Richmond, Indiana, Hicksite Meeting House, December 2ⁿᵈ
        1859*, 1859, 4½ x 7½ in.

2.33   Lefevre James Cranstone, *Richmond, Indiana, Main Street*, 1859, 4½ x 7½ in.

2.34   Lefevre James Cranstone, *Richmond, Indiana*, 1859, 4½ x 7½ in.

2.35   Lefevre James Cranstone, *Richmond, Indiana, Public School*, 1859, 4½ x 7½ in.

2.36   Lefevre James Cranstone, *Richmond, Indiana*, 1859, 4½ x 7½ in.

2.37   Lefevre James Cranstone, *Richmond, Indiana, Seventh Street*, 1859, 4½ x 7½ in.

2.38   Lefevre James Cranstone, *Richmond, Indiana*, 1859, 4½ x 7½ in.

2.39   Lefevre James Cranstone, *Near Richmond, Indiana, January 2nd1860*, 1860, 4½ x 7½ in.

2.40   Lefevre James Cranstone, *Nr. Richmond, Indiana. January 3rd1860*, 1860, 4½ x 7½ in.

2.41   Lefevre James Cranstone, *Richmond, Indiana, Episcopal Church*, 1860, 4½ x 7½ in.

2.42   Lefevre James Cranstone, *Richmond, Indiana*, 1860, 4½ x 7½ in.

2.43   Lefevre James Cranstone, *Richmond, Indiana, Presbyterian Church*, 1860, 4½ x 7½ in.

2.44   Lefevre James Cranstone, *Covington, Kentucky. January 1860* 1860, 4½ x 7½ in.

2.45   Lefevre James Cranstone, *Newport, Kentucky. January 10th 1860*, 1860, 4½ x 7½ in.

2.46   Lefevre James Cranstone, *The President's House, Washington. March 1860*, 1860, 4½ x 7½ in.

2.47   Lefevre James Cranstone, *Washington March, 1860* 1860, 4½ x 7½ in.

2.48   Lefevre James Cranstone, *Washington*, 1860, 4½ x 7½ in.

2.49   Lefevre James Cranstone, *Washington*, 1860, 4½ x 7½ in.

2.50   Lefevre James Cranstone, *Civilization by Greenough, at the Capitol, Washington*, 1860, 4½ x 7½ in.

2.51   Lefevre James Cranstone, *Columbus by Persico at the Capitol, Washington*, 1860, 4½ x 7½ in.

2.52   Lefevre James Cranstone, *Washington, City Hall*, 1860, 4½ x 7½ in.

2.53   Lefevre James Cranstone, *Washington Treasury Department*, 1860, 4½ x 7½ in.

2.54   Lefevre James Cranstone, *Washington, Post Office*, 1860, 4½ x 7½ in.

2.55   Lefevre James Cranstone, *Washington, Patent Office*, 1860, 4½ x 7½ in.

2.56   Lefevre James Cranstone, *State House, Richmond, Virginia*, 1860, 4½ x 7½ in.

2.57   Lefevre James Cranstone, *Monument to Washington, Richmond, Virginia*, 1860, 4½ x 7½ in.

2.58   Lefevre James Cranstone, *James River & Canal, Richmond, Virginia*, 1860, 4½ x 7½ in.

2.59   Lefevre James Cranstone, *Richmond, Virginia*, 1860, 4½ x 7½ in.

2.60   Lefevre James Cranstone, *Richmond, Virginia*, 1860, 4½ x 7½ in.

2.61   Lefevre James Cranstone, *St. John's Church, Richmond, Virginia*, 1860, 4½ x 7½ in.

2.62   Lefevre James Cranstone, *James River, nr. Richmond*, 1860, 4½ x 7½ in.

2.63   Lefevre James Cranstone, *West Point, York River*, 1860, 4½ x 7½ in.

2.64   Lefevre James Cranstone, *Near Williamsburg, Virginia*, 1860, 4½ x 7½ in.

2.65   Lefevre James Cranstone, *Near Williamsburg, Virginia*, 1860, 4½ x 7½ in.

2.66   Lefevre James Cranstone, *Near Bigler's Mills, Virginia. March 1860*, 1860, 4½ x 7½ in.

2.67   Lefevre James Cranstone, *Near Bigler's Mills, Virginia*, 1860, 4 ½ x 7½ in.

2.68   Lefevre James Cranstone, *Rippon Hall, Virginia*, 1860, 4½ x 7½ in.

2.69   Lefevre James Cranstone, *Rippon Hall, Nr. Williamsburg, Virginia*, 1860, 4½ x 7½ in.

2.70   Lefevre James Cranstone, *York River, Virginia*, 1860, 4½ x 7½ in.

2.71   Lefevre James Cranstone, *Bigler's Mills, Virginia*, 1860, 4½ x 7½ in.

2.72   Lefevre James Cranstone, *Bigler's Mills, York River, Virginia*, 1860, 4½ x 7½ in.

2.73   Lefevre James Cranstone, *Porto Bello, Virginia, formerly the residence of Lord Dunmore*, 1860, 4½ x 7½ in.

2.74   Lefevre James Cranstone, *Episcopal Church, Williamsburg, Virginia*, 1860, 4½ x 7½ in.

2.75   Lefevre James Cranstone, *Court House, Williamsburg, Virginia, March 1860*, 1860, 4½ x 7½ in.

2.76   Lefevre James Cranstone, *Williamsburg, Virginia, March 1860*, 1860, 4½ x 7½ in.

2.77   Lefevre James Cranstone, *Insane asylum, Williamsburg, Virginia*, 1860, 4½ x 7½ in.

2.78   Lefevre James Cranstone, *The Old Palace, Williamsburg, Virginia*, 1860, 4½ x 7½ in.

2.79   Lefevre James Cranstone, *William and Mary College, Williamsburg, Virginia*, 1860, 4½ x 7½ in.

2.80   Lefevre James Cranstone, *Harper's Ferry, Virginia*, 1860, 4½ x 7½ in.

2.81   Lefevre James Cranstone, *Harper's Ferry, Virginia*, 1860, 4½ x 7½ in.

2.82   Lefevre James Cranstone, *Harper's Ferry, Virginia*, 1860, 4½ x 7½ in.

2.83   Lefevre James Cranstone, *Wheeling, Virginia*, 1860, 4½ x 7½ in.

2.84   Lefevre James Cranstone, *Ohio River, Wheeling*, 1860, 4½ x 7½ in.

2.85   Lefevre James Cranstone, *Near Wheeling, Virginia*, 1860, 4½ x 7½ in.

2.86   Lefevre James Cranstone, *Wheeling Creek, Virginia*, 1860, 4½ x 7½ in.

2.87   Lefevre James Cranstone, *Nr. Wheeling, Virginia*, 1860, 4½ x 7½ in.

2.88   Lefevre James Cranstone, *St. Clairsville Road Ohio*, 1860, 4½ x 7½ in.

2.89   Lefevre James Cranstone, *Ohio River*, 1860, 4½ x 7½ in.

2.90   Lefevre James Cranstone, *Do not steal the papers*, 1860, 4½ x 7½ in.

2.91   Lefevre James Cranstone, *Cleveland, Ohio*, 1860, 4½ x 7½ in.

2.92   Lefevre James Cranstone, *Buffalo*, 1860, 4½ x 7½ in.

2.93   Lefevre James Cranstone, *Buffalo*, 1860, 4½ x 7½ in.

2.94   Lefevre James Cranstone, *Buffalo*, 1860, 4½ x 7½ in.

2.95   Lefevre James Cranstone, *Falls of Niagara-From Chippewa 3 miles,* 1860, 4½ x 7½ in.

2.96   Lefevre James Cranstone, *Niagara*, 1860, 4½ x 7½ in.

2.97   Lefevre James Cranstone, *The Falls of Niagara The American Falls*, 1860, 4½ x 7½ in.

2.98   Lefevre James Cranstone, *At the Falls of Niagara*, 1860, 4½ x 7½ in.

2.99   Lefevre James Cranstone, *Falls of Niagara – The Rapids*, 1860, 4½ x 7½ in.

2.100   Lefevre James Cranstone, *Falls of Niagara*, 1860, 4½ x 7½ in.

2.101   Lefevre James Cranstone, *Falls of Niagara*, 1860, 4½ x 7½ in.

2.102   Lefevre James Cranstone, *Suspension Bridge Niagara*, 1860, 4½ x 7½ in.

2.103   Lefevre James Cranstone, *Falls of Niagara. Canada side,* 1860, 4½ x 7½ in.

2.104   Lefevre James Cranstone, *Niagara,* 1860, 4½ x 7½ in.

2.105   Lefevre James Cranstone, *Greenwood Cemetery, Brooklyn, Long Island,* 1860, 4½ x 7½ in.

2.106   Lefevre James Cranstone, *Castle Garden Depot, New York,* 1860, 4½ x 7½ in.

2.107   Lefevre James Cranstone, *Off Queenstown, Ireland,* 1860, double panels, 4½ x 15 in.

Chapter 3

3.1   Lefevre James Cranstone, *Slave Auction, Virginia,* 1863, oil on fabric, 13 x 21 in. Courtesy, Virginia Historical Society, Richmond, Virginia.

Chapter 4

4.1   Lefevre James Cranstone, *Court House of 1770,* 1860, watercolor on paper, 7 ¾ x 12 ¾ in. Courtesy, Colonial Williamsburg Foundation.

4.2   Lefevre James Cranstone, *Richmond, Va.,* 1860, watercolor on paper, 7 ½ x 11 ¾ in. Courtesy, Virginia Historical Society, Richmond, Virginia.

4.3   Lefevre James Cranstone, *York River, Virginia, Biglers Mill – With Artist and a Man Standing Behind Him,* 1860, watercolor on paper, 6 ¼ x 13 in. Courtesy, Virginia Museum of Fine Arts, Richmond. The Paul Mellon Collection.

4.4   Lefevre James Cranstone, *Richmond, Indiana, Seventh St,* 1860, watercolor on paper, 5 ½ x 13 1/8 in. Courtesy, Indiana Historical Society.

4.5   Lefevre James Cranstone, *White House, Rear View, 1860,* 1860, watercolor on paper, 7 1/16 x 12 7/16 in. Courtesy, "The White House" (249), Washington, D.C.

4.6   Lefevre James Cranstone, *Near Wheeling, West Virginia,* 1860, watercolor on paper, 13 ½ x 18 ¾ in. Courtesy, Senator & Mrs. John D. Rockefeller IV Collection.

4.7   Lefevre James Cranstone, *Woodland Road in (West) Virginia,* 1859, watercolor on paper, 6 ½ x 1115/16 in. Courtesy, Museum of Fine Arts, Boston.

4.8   Lefevre James Cranstone, *Mills Near Wheeling, Virginia,* 1860, watercolor on paper, 6 3/8 x 12 ¼ in. Courtesy, Oglebay Institute Mansion Museum, Wheeling, West Virginia.

4.9   Lefevre James Cranstone, *View of Cutting Ice,* 1860, watercolor on paper, 6 x 12 3/8 in. Courtesy, Richmond Art Museum, Richmond, Indiana.

Chapter 5

5.1   Lefevre James Cranstone, *Portrait of Sarah Pollard Cranstone,* 1841, 11 x 12 ¼ in., oil on fabric. Courtesy, Mrs. Sheila Gander.

5.2   Lefevre James Cranstone, *Joseph Cranstone* and *Maria Cranstone*, c. 1840, 3 ¼ x 2 ¾ in., watercolors. Courtesy, Mrs. Sheila Gander.

5.3   Gadebridge Park Bridge, Hemel Hempstead, England, 2002, photo. Courtesy, the author.

5.4   Lefevre James Cranstone, *St. Mary's Church, Hemel Hempstead*, c. 1840, watercolor on paper, 10 ¼ x 12.0 in. Courtesy, Mrs. Sheila Gander.

5.5   Lefevre James Cranstone, *Waiting at the Station*, 1850, oil on canvas, 26 x 42 in., whereabouts unknown.

5.6   Lefevre James Cranstone, *Swarthmore Meeting House*, 1847, watercolor on paper, 12 ¼ x 8 ½ in. Courtesy, David Cranstone and Dacorum Heritage Trust Ltd, Berkhamsted, England.

5.7   Lefevre James Cranstone, *Figures on the Beach at Broadstairs*, c.1850, watercolor on paper, 4 ¾ x 7.0 in., whereabouts unknown.

5.8   Lefevre James Cranstone, *Remains of the Old Bury House, Hemel Hempstead*, 1849, copper plate engraving, 8.5 x 4.0 in. Courtesy, David Cranstone and Dacorum Heritage Trust Ltd, Berkhamsted, England.

5.9   Lefevre James Cranstone, *Clock House, St. Albans*, 1849, copper plate engraving, 6.0 x 5 ½ in. Courtesy, David Cranstone and Dacorum Heritage Trust Ltd, Berkhamsted, England.

5.10   Lefevre James Cranstone, *Netley Abbey*, 1849, copper plate engraving, 7.5 x 5 ½ in. Courtesy, David Cranstone and Dacorum Heritage Trust Ltd, Berkhamsted, England.

5.11   Lefevre James Cranstone, *Near the Hoe, Plymouth*, 1849, copper plate engraving, 7.0 x 5.0 in. Courtesy, David Cranstone and Dacorum Heritage Trust Ltd, Berkhamsted, England.

5.12   Lefevre James Cranstone, *Cottage Interior*, 1849, copper plate engraving, 6 ½ x 5 ¾ in. Courtesy, David Cranstone and Dacorum Heritage Trust Ltd, Berkhamsted, England.

5.13   Lefevre James Cranstone, *Hemel Hempstead Market Place*, c. 1855, oil on fabric, 15 ½ x 12 ½ in. Courtesy, David Cranstone and Dacorum Heritage Trust Ltd, Berkhamsted, England.

5.14   Lillia Messenger Cranstone, c. 1859, daguerreotype. Courtesy, Richmond Art Museum, Richmond, Indiana.

5.15   The "White House," Hemel Hempstead, England, 2002, photo. Courtesy, the author.

Chapter 6

6.1   Lillia Cranstone Tombstone, Heath Lane Cemetery, Hemel Hempstead, England, 2001, photo. Courtesy, the author.

6.2   *The Clipper Ship Ann Duthie, Nearing Sydney Heads,* 1869, Illustrated Sydney News, Jan 21, 1869. Courtesy, Mitchell Library, State Library of New South Wales, Australia.

6.3   Lefevre James Cranstone, *Fairy Bower, Manly, Sydney*, 1883, pen and ink drawing, 12 ¾ x 9 ¼ in. Courtesy, David Cranstone and Dacorum Heritage Trust Ltd, Berkhamsted, England.

6.4   Lefevre James Cranstone, *Sydney Harbor*, 1883, pen and ink drawing, 12 ¾ x 8.0 in. Courtesy, David Cranstone and Dacorum Heritage Trust Ltd, Berkhamsted, England.

6.5   *Parramatta River, Sydney*, 1883, pen and ink drawing, 12 ¾ x 9.0 in. Courtesy, David Cranstone and Dacorum Heritage Trust Ltd, Berkhamsted, England.

6.6   Lefevre James Cranstone, *Illustrated Poem by Thomson*, c. 1865, watercolor, 9.0 x 11 ¼ in. Courtesy, Collection: John Oxley Library, State Library of Queensland, Australia.

6.7   Lefevre James Cranstone, *Retro, Queensland*, c.1885, pen and ink drawing, 12 ¾ x 9.0 in. Courtesy, David Cranstone and Dacorum Heritage Trust Ltd, Berkhamsted, England.

6.8   Lefevre James Cranstone, *Fairview, Wolfang, Queensland*, c.1885, pen and ink drawing, 12 ¾ x 9.0 in. Courtesy, David Cranstone and Dacorum Heritage Trust Ltd, Berkhamsted, England.

6.9   Lefevre James Cranstone, *Near Clermont*, c.1885, pen and ink drawing, 12 ¾ x 9.0 in. Courtesy, David Cranstone and Dacorum Heritage Trust Ltd, Berkhamsted, England.

6.10   Lefevre James Cranstone, *Brisbane – Leichhardt St,* c. 1890, pen and ink drawing, 5 7/8 x 8 5/8 in. Courtesy, Collection: John Oxley Library, State Library of Queensland, Australia.

6.11   Lefevre James Cranstone, *Brisbane,* c. 1890, pen and ink drawing, 5 7/8 x 8 5/8 in. Courtesy, Collection: John Oxley Library, State Library of Queensland, Australia.

6.12   Lefevre James Cranstone, *Milton – Brisbane,* c. 1890, 5 7/8 x 8 5/8 in. Courtesy, Collection: John Oxley Library, State Library of Queensland, Australia.

6.13   Tombstone of Lefevre James Cranstone, Brisbane General Cemetery, Brisbane, Australia, 2002, photo. Courtesy, the author.

FOREWORD

Nearly 300 Cranstone watercolor drawings were acquired by Indiana University in 1944—a purchase from the British antiquarian firm, Henry Stevens' Son & Stiles. Although the work of a British artist, the drawings held particular Indiana interest because of the thirty-five sketches of Richmond, Indiana, executed between November 1859 and January 1860. Other Cranstone sketches present in the Lilly Library collection include a few made by him while aboard ship sailing to America; about ninety of or around Wheeling, West Virginia, several showing the Ohio River with steamboats present; over 100 of various places in Virginia including in particular Richmond, Harper's Ferry, West Point, and Williamsburg; fourteen of Washington D.C. and area; eight of Ohio and Kentucky locales; and thirty-five of New York state, especially around Niagara Falls.

During the nearly sixty years in Indiana University's possession, selections from the entire collection have been displayed in such disparate venues as the Richmond (Indiana) Art Museum (at least three times since 1962), the Oglebay Institute Mansion Museum in Wheeling, West Virginia, in 1984, and the Virginia Historical Society in Richmond, Virginia, in 2000.

Meanwhile many scholars and researchers have also been interested in the drawings. Each use or inquiry included questions about Lefevre Cranstone. Exactly who was he, when did he live, where did he come from and why was he in America at all; and most importantly from the Hoosier point of view, why did he visit and make sketches of buildings and the countryside around Richmond, Indiana? We, the staff in the Lilly Library, were never able to answer such questions in a thorough or even satisfactory way. Although we knew he was visiting a cousin in Richmond in 1859, many of the other questions went unanswered; yet the drawings were studied, exhibited, reproduced and of course credited as the work of one Lefevre Cranstone, 19th century British artist.

In 2001, along came Don Smith of Williamsburg, Virginia, inquiring about the drawings and the artist. And while he too was interested in reproducing the works, he wanted even more to know about the artist. Who was he, what led to his producing these American scenes, why had he come to America? His curiosity led to a two-year quest for the life and story of Lefevre James Cranstone. The results of that search and the information discovered are presented in this volume.

The story of a heretofore unknown and unrecognized 19th century artist is revealed here, appropriately and amply illustrated with his own works, including many of the sketches that document his brief visit to Indiana and the southern

United States, virtually on the eve of the Civil War, that now reside in the Lilly Library of Indiana University.

Saundra Taylor
Curator of Manuscripts
Lilly Library
Indiana University, Bloomington, Indiana

ACKNOWLEDGMENTS

I have many people to thank for the time, help and advice they provided in helping me gather and present in a coherent and readable form this information on the life and art of Lefevre James Cranstone. In addition to the countless hours my wife Jan has spent assisting with research and providing insightful comments, I am also indebted to my daughters, Therese Camp and Kari Smith for reading the drafts and providing very helpful suggestions. My sister, Maria Smith, and brother, Nelson Smith, also provided invaluable assistance during the research and writing phases. Jennifer Whitehead, my niece, and her husband Pete Whitehead's suggestions from their artist's perspectives have also helped to improve the presentation and readability of the book.

The background information and images of Cranstone and his art were researched and collected on three continents thanks primarily to the assistance and interest of many friends, new and old, who each showed a passion for art and research as well as an interest in seeing this story told.

In the United States, I'm very grateful to Saundra Taylor and Chris Harter, Lilly Library, Indiana University, Bloomington, Indiana; Kathleen Glynn and Shaun Dingwerth, Richmond Art Museum, Richmond, Indiana; Ms. Jessie Turner, Richmond, Indiana; Susan Sutton, Indiana Historical Society, Indianapolis, Indiana; Travis Zeik, Holly McClusky, and Maureen Zambito of the Oglebay Institute Mansion Museum, Wheeling, West Virginia; Mary Moore, Wheeling Jesuit College, Wheeling, West Virginia; Renea Peake, Wheeling, West Virginia; R. Jeanne Cobb, Bethany College, Bethany, West Virginia; Lisa Hancock and Sharon Casale, Virginia Museum of Fine Arts, Richmond, Virginia; William S. Rasmussen, Virginia Historical Society, Richmond, Virginia; Sue Welsh Reed, Boston Museum of Fine Arts, Boston, Massachusetts; Senator John D. Rockefeller, IV, West Virginia and staff member Christina Ryan, Washington, D.C.; Meg J. Perlman, Curator, Senator & Mrs. John D. Rockefeller IV Collection, New York, New York; Lydia Dufour, Frick Art Reference Library, New York, N.Y.; and Laura Pass Barry, Donna Sheppard and Joann Proper of the Colonial Williamsburg Foundation, Williamsburg, Virginia.

For England, they are David Cranstone, the great grandnephew of Lefevre James Cranstone, Gateshead, who provided invaluable assistance; Sheila Gander, Hove, grand-niece of the artist; Matt Wheeler, Dacorum Heritage Trust, Berkhamsted; Elizabeth Buteux, Hemel Hempstead; Elizabeth King and Andrew Potter of the Royal Academy of Arts, London; and Lucy Ducat-Hamersley of Sotheby's London.

For Australia, they are Ian Dudgeon of Canberra, George Knox of Brisbane, and

Dianne F. Byrne and Kaye E. Nardella of the John Oxley Library in Brisbane.

Finally, I would also like to thank Robert H. Pruett, publisher, Brandylane Publishers, Inc., for the outstanding job he did in shepherding both the manuscript and the author through the publication process.

INTRODUCTION

Conducting research on an eighteenth century Tidewater Virginia plantation may seem a strange way to stumble across a relatively unknown nineteenth century British artist. It happened, however, when I was conducting research on Ripon Hall, a plantation on the York River near Williamsburg built in the late seventeenth century by Edmund Jenings, a member of the Colonial Council and Acting Governor of the Colony of Virginia from 1706-1710.

It all started when a routine search for information about Ripon Hall turned up a reference to a watercolor painting by that title attributed to the British artist, Lefevre James Cranstone. The painting, part of the Virginia Historical Society Paul Mellon Collection, depicts the Ripon Hall area as Cranstone viewed it in May 1860. Further inquiry revealed that a collection of 296 watercolor sketches made by Cranstone during his nine-month visit to America in 1859-1860 resides in the Lilly Library at Indiana University in Bloomington, Indiana. Later, I learned that additional, more detailed watercolors based on these sketches can be found not only at the Virginia Historical Society but also at the White House, the Indiana Historical Society, Museum of Fine Arts, Boston, the Virginia Museum of Fine Arts, Oglebay Institute Mansion Museum, Richmond, Indiana Art Museum and as part of other art collections.

It was clear the Ripon Hall painting was rendered by a talented artist and exciting to realize the Lilly Library and other institutions possessed so many of his sketches. Who was Lefevre James Cranstone? Why had he visited the United States? Where had he visited? I could find only the barest and sometimes contradictory information on Cranstone in major art reference books referring mostly to paintings exhibited in England during the nineteenth century, the sketch collection at the Lilly Library, and his eventual immigration to Australia. It seemed plausible that more information about him existed, so visits to libraries, historical societies and museums in Great Britain, Australia, and the United States followed.

This book contains the interesting and detailed results of my research on the life and art of Lefevre James Cranstone. His story describes a versatile, talented artist who grew up in the small town of Hemel Hempstead twenty miles northwest of London and who at age eighteen began his formal art training at the Royal Academy of Arts in London. Cranstone's life and interests took him to three continents where he painted and exhibited for more than fifty years.

1

Journey to America

About August 27, 1859, Lefevre James Cranstone set forth on a journey to America that would last more than ten months. The artist left his two children, four-month old son, Frederick, and three year old son, William at home in the care of his wife, Lillia. After traveling overland from Hemel Hempstead to Liverpool, Cranstone boarded the steamer *Kangaroo* for the twenty day voyage to New York.[1]

1.1 *Lefevre James Cranstone*, c. 1859, photograph, Palladium-Item, April 9, 1951. Courtesy, Palladium-Item, Richmond, Indiana.

The ship departed Liverpool on August 31ˢᵗ and picked up passengers in Queenstown (now Cobh), Ireland on September 2ⁿᵈ. After departing Queenstown, it called at Halifax, Nova Scotia fourteen days later for about eight hours to take on a re-supply of coal.

1.2 *Steamer Kangaroo*, built 1853, photograph. Courtesy, Mariners' Museum, Newport News, VA

When the ship arrived at the Port of New York City on September 19, 1859 with its cargo of merchandise and 321 passengers, Captain James M. Jeffrey provided the required list of names, ages, sex, occupations, countries of origin, and country where the passengers intended to become inhabitants.[2] The list contains some revealing information. First, the entry for Lefevre Cranstone inexplicably cites his first name as Laurence and his country of origin as Scotland although entries for his age as thirty-seven years old and occupation as artist are correct. The spelling of Cranstone's first name as Laurence rather than Lefevre might represent the clerk miscopying his name. Listing Scotland instead of England as the country of origin, however, is a puzzle.

For all 321 passengers, the list states the "U.S.A." is where they intended to live. This designation next to Cranstone's name may be the result of the clerk filling out the form, assuming America was the final destination for all passengers.

The passenger list also revealed Cranstone had a traveling companion. Directly below Lefevre's name is that of his younger brother, Alfred Cranstone, age twenty-one, occupation artist, country of origin, Scotland, with "U.S.A" written in as the country to which he intended to immigrate. Family history notes that Alfred, born July 17, 1839, was the thirteenth of the fifteen Cranstone children.[3]

1.3 *Frances, William Henry, Eliza, Alfred and Lefevre James Cranstone*, Hemel Hempstead, England, c.1860, photograph, D/Ece/F41. Courtesy, Hertfordshire Archives & Local Studies, Hertford, England

What brought Cranstone and his brother to America? Did they really come to explore the possibility of eventually immigrating? Alternatively, as the occupation for both Cranstones is listed as artist, it could have been a field trip for Alfred who most likely studied art under Lefevre. In his book *Early Art and Artists in West Virginia: An Introduction and Biographical Dictionary*, John A. Cuthbert discusses the many British artists who visited America to capture its scenic beauty through art. Perhaps, this was their objective?[4]

The brothers also had personal reasons for the trip since they stayed with relatives on at least two occasions. During a month long visit to Richmond, Indiana they visited William Lefevre, Jr., a cousin on their mother's side. Later, while in the Williamsburg, Virginia area for over a month, they resided with another cousin on their father's side of the family.[5] The brothers also spent a total of five months in and around Wheeling, West Virginia area on three separate occasions. During those visits, there is the possibility they also stayed with relatives or family friends.

Cranstone's Itinerary

Unfortunately, no diary of Cranstone's visit has been found, but while a diary describing his trip would be most helpful, it isn't necessary since a pleasant substitute is available in the watercolor sketches he prepared. Rather than using words, Cranstone captured his itinerary using his artistic talent, thus providing a lasting visual record we can use to recreate his journey.

Many of the sketches done during the journey are available for study. In addition, he also prepared a number of larger, more complete watercolors and at least two oil paintings based on his sketches. The Lilly Library at Indiana University has 296 of his watercolor sketches in their possession. The Indiana University Foundation purchased this collection for the university in 1944 from the very prominent antiquarian book selling firm, Henry Stevens' Son and Stiles of London.[6] The sketches were initially offered for sale during the summer of 1928 by Lefevre's nephew, Arthur Cranstone, and subsequently in the fall by his representative B. F. Stevens & Brown Ltd. At the time the collection was described as consisting of 304 original watercolor sketches by Lefevre James Cranstone bound in old half Morocco, the drawings being mounted two on a page.

Coincidentally, there was interest in purchasing the collection in 1928 by a number of Americans. In June 1928, Mrs. Winifred Comstock Bowman of London and originally from Richmond, Indiana, inspected the collection.[7] Later, her parents, Mr. and Mrs. Paul Comstock, visited London in October 1928 and also viewed the collection.[8] The asking price was £500, about $1,900 at the time, which the Comstocks considered too high. Negotiations to purchase separately only the thirty-five sketches related to Richmond, Indiana failed when Arthur Cranstone refused to break up the collection. The Comstocks then attempted to interest others in Indiana to join them in sharing the expense for the entire collection, but they were unsuccessful.

The existence of the sketches was brought to the attention of the general public through an article in *The Art Weekly* of London of September 13, 1928.[9] B. F. Stevens & Brown, Ltd. tried to develop interest in purchasing the collection by sending letters to the Library of Congress, and because of the inclusion of sketches related to Williamsburg, Virginia, to John D. Rockefeller, Jr. of New York[10] and J. A. C. Chandler, President of the College of William & Mary, Williamsburg, Virginia.[11] While the College did not pursue the purchase of the collection, the Reverend William A. R. Goodwin, a faculty member, rector of the historic Bruton Parish Church and the person who single-handedly convinced Rockefeller to finance the restoration of Williamsburg's colonial area, brought the opportunity to the attention of Rockefeller's representative, Colonel Arthur Woods, President of Colonial Williamsburg, Inc.[12] In the end, the asking price of £500 and the unwillingness of Cranstone's nephew to break up the collection, discouraged the prospective American buyers.

The entire set of sketches was still owned by B. F. Stevens & Brown, Ltd. when they were again offered for sale in their 1942 catalogue.[13] Interestingly, the number offered was now given as 312, up for an unexplained reason from the 304 originally offered in 1928. Even this earlier number seemed to be questionable as only 296 sketches were present on the original list provided in 1928 to Rockefeller by B. F. Stevens & Brown, Ltd. In 1942, the price for the sketches was now listed as $1,500.00. As noted earlier, two years later, thanks to the Indiana University Foundation, the collection was at Indiana University.

2

Places Visited, 1859-1860

We can follow the footsteps Cranstone took during his trip through the eastern part of America as recreated through the 296 sketches in the Lilly Library collection.[14] To some, it may seem quite a feat that Cranstone prepared almost 300 sketches over a ten month period, an average of one or more a day. In fact, on some days, he did four or five sketches. Concerning artist's materials such as sketchbooks and watercolor painting supplies, he most likely brought them from England rather than having to depend on purchasing them on his journey. Each sketch is 4 ½" x 7½" in size and prepared on only one side of a sketchbook page. Double pages were also occasionally used to prepare fourteen panoramas. At some point after returning home, the pages of the sketchbooks were separated and the individual sketches adhered two to a page of a larger scrapbook. It was in this form that the Cranstone collection was first offered for sale in 1928. At some point, this scrapbook was dismantled and the collection today at the Lilly Library consists of a specially made box containing these separated pages.

A few comments about notations found on the sketches: some have a specific day, date and place appended, while only the month and general location of the scene are noted on others. As a result, identical titles are present on a number of the sketches Cranstone prepared in a geographical area.

Numbers are written in the upper right hand corners of certain sketches suggesting that two different subsets were prepared for an unknown purpose. Although the subsets have been recreated, their content and order did not shed any light on why they were assembled. However, the absence of some consecutive numbers in the series does suggest that several sketches were removed from the original collection prior to its sale.

Liverpool to New York City

Cranstone recorded the start of his journey on September 1, 1859 by sketching a panorama of the Welsh skyline showing hills and lighthouses in the distance. He prepared similar scenes off the entrance to Queenstown, Ireland and near the south coast of Ireland.

2.1 *The Kangaroo Sept. 2nd,* wash on paper, 1859, 4½ x 7½ in. Courtesy, The Lilly Library, Indiana University, Bloomington, Indiana

During the voyage across the Atlantic, Cranstone drew the crowded conditions endured by the 282 men, women, and children traveling in steerage in a series of sketches.

2.2 *Deck of the Kangaroo*, wash on paper, 1859, 4½ x 7½ in. Courtesy, The Lilly Library, Indiana University, Bloomington, Indiana

A brief stop in Halifax, Nova Scotia on September 16, allowed Cranstone to paint four scenes of downtown Halifax. He rendered another of neighboring Dartmouth as the ship passed this city returning to sea.

2.3 *Market Place, Halifax*, wash on paper, 1859, 4½ x 7½ in. Courtesy, The Lilly Library, Indiana University, Bloomington, Indiana

2.4 *Halifax, N.S.,* wash on paper, 1859, 4½ x 7½ in. Courtesy, The Lilly Library, Indiana University, Bloomington, Indiana

2.5 *Dartmouth, Nova Scotia, September 16th 1859,* wash on paper, 1859, 4½ x 7½ in. Courtesy, The Lilly Library, Indiana University, Bloomington, Indiana

The *Kangaroo* anchored in New York harbor on September 19th and the passengers were ferried to Castle Garden at the southern tip of Manhattan to go through immigration.

9

2.6 *The Kangaroo Landing Passengers, New York, September 19th*, wash on paper, 1859, 4½ x 7½ in. Courtesy, The Lilly Library, Indiana University, Bloomington, Indiana

Wheeling, West Virginia to Cincinnati, Ohio

After Cranstone left New York, the first recorded stop in his sketches is Wheeling, Virginia. (As West Virginia did not become a separate state until 1863, Cranstone labeled towns such as Wheeling, Parkersburg and Harper's Ferry as Virginia on his sketches). He stayed in the Wheeling area three different times for almost five of his nine month stay in the United States. Whom did he stay with in Wheeling? Family notes suggest he stayed somewhere on his trip with an uncle named William Kentish.[15] A thorough search of Wheeling records and the 1860 Federal Census revealed no such person.

If it wasn't a relative, perhaps Cranstone stayed with a family friend or an artist who lived in the area? Clues were sought in the ninety-four sketches near Wheeling he prepared during his three visits to the area. A close inspection of these sketches indicates Cranstone spent the majority of his time in rural areas northeast of the city. There is a noticeable lack of sketches of the downtown, industrial, or residential districts of Wheeling but an abundance depicting farmhouses, country roads, fields, and distant views of the Ohio River. The emphasis on rural scenes is quite different from those Cranstone did during his visits to other cities. For example, his sketches of Richmond, Indiana and Washington, D. C. highlight his ability to draw

10

architecturally accurate renderings of churches, homes, and public buildings, a legacy from his studies at the Royal Academy. Perhaps, Cranstone had recorded such buildings in Wheeling and presented them as tokens of gratitude for the hospitality extended him during his visits there?

A careful investigation was made of Wheeling vicinity inhabitants of the time to discover if any could have been Cranstone's host. One area of habitation was northeast of Wheeling along the National Road as it wound along Wheeling Creek past Fulton, Pleasant Valley, and Elm Grove. Of the residents of this area, Asa C. Partridge, listed as an "artist" in the 1860 census and owner of a popular photography shop in Wheeling, emerged as a strong candidate. Originally from Vermont, Partridge settled in Wheeling in 1848 and married Elizabeth Ann Philbrick there October 17, 1852. Their home was on the National Road near Fulton.

What could have brought these two men together? The connection may have been the school Cranstone's wife, Lillia, ran in Hemel Hempstead. The 1861 British Census revealed two of her students, Mary Runnels, age eleven and Lilley T. Runnels, age five were American citizens. A third student, Washington Runnels, their four-year old brother, was listed as Scottish.[16] Their ages and citizenships indicate the children's parents previously lived in America and returned to Scotland for the birth of their third child. The connection to Asa Partridge may be through his wife, the former Elizabeth Philbrick, the daughter of Joseph Philbrick and Nancy B. Runnels. Thus, it is possible the father of the Runnels children was an uncle or cousin of Elizabeth Philbrick Partridge, who upon learning of Cranstone's trip to America arranged the introduction to Asa Partridge.

In addition to his watercolor sketches, given his earlier experience painting portraits in England, Cranstone may also have worked with Partridge doing portraiture of some of Fulton's leading citizens. Portraits from prominent families of the period such as the Woods, Marshall, and Thompson families may possibly contain the Cranstone signature.

Cranstone's first sketch of the area depicts the famous McCulloch's Leap in North Wheeling. This site earned its name when Major Samuel McCulloch made a miraculous getaway on horseback down the steep eastern slope of Wheeling hill while being pursued by a band of marauding Native Americans as he was leading forty-five soldiers to the relief of besieged Fort Henry in 1777.[17]

11

2.7 McCulloch's Leap, Wheeling, Va. September 1859, wash on paper, 1859, 4½ x 7½ in. Courtesy, The Lilly Library, Indiana University, Bloomington, Indiana

Cranstone captured picturesque views of farmhouses and the stone viaduct and tunnel of the Hempfield and Wheeling Railroad line. Over the next few weeks, he recorded scenes of the local countryside including the small village of Fulton and houses and mills along Wheeling Creek.

2.8 Tunnel, Hempfield & Wheeling Line, Va. October 2nd 1859, wash on paper, 1859, 4½ x 7½ in. Courtesy, The Lilly Library, Indiana University, Bloomington, Indiana

2.9 *Railway Bridge near Wheeling, Va. October 2ⁿᵈ 1859*, wash on paper, 1859, 4½ x 7½ in. Courtesy, The Lilly Library, Indiana University, Bloomington, Indiana

2.10 *Methodist Church & School House, Fulton, Virginia*, wash on paper, 1859, 4½ x 7½ in. Courtesy, The Lilly Library, Indiana University, Bloomington, Indiana

Cranstone occasionally prepared a more fully rendered sketch with increased details and coloring. One, my personal favorite, shows an African-American woman, shawl over her head and shoulders, carrying a basket walking along a forested country road. Cranstone's detail captures the natural beauty of stones, road surface and fully leafed trees adjoining the road in a brown wash. The woman's position at the center of the sketch highlights her presence as she makes her way home, basket in hand.

2.11 *Nr. Wheeling, Virginia*, wash on paper, 1859, 4½ x 7½ in. Courtesy, The Lilly Library, Indiana University, Bloomington, Indiana

Other sketches depict fishermen intent on landing the big one while fishing on Wheeling Creek on the outskirts of Wheeling.

2.12 *Nr. Wheeling, Virginia*, wash on paper, 1859, 4½ x 7½ in. Courtesy, The Lilly Library, Indiana University, Bloomington, Indiana

2.13 *Near Wheeling, Virginia*, wash on paper, 1859, 4½ x 7½ in. Courtesy, The Lilly Library, Indiana University, Bloomington, Indiana

Cranstone also painted the Ohio River Valley from high on a hillside on the West Virginia side of the river. This sketch depicts the river with Lower Twin Island in the background and a dirt road and split rail fence in the foreground.

2.14 *Ohio River, Nr. Wheeling*, wash on paper, 1859, 4½ x 7½ in. Courtesy, The Lilly Library, Indiana University, Bloomington, Indiana

Yielding what seemed to be a never resting paintbrush Cranstone continued recording scenes of the area. At one point the artist ventured to the edge of the Ohio River to paint a passing steamboat. Later, Cranstone returned to sketch different perspectives of McCulloch's Leap and the Hempfield and Wheeling railroad viaduct.

2.15 *The Ohio River,* wash on paper, 1859, 4½ x 7½ in. Courtesy, The Lilly Library, Indiana University, Bloomington, Indiana

2.16 *McCulloch's Leap, Wheeling, Virginia,* wash on paper, 1859, 4½ x 7½ in. Courtesy, The Lilly Library, Indiana University, Bloomington, Indiana

2.17 *Hempfield Railway, Nr. Wheeling Va.* wash on paper, 1859, 4½ x 7½ in. Courtesy, The Lilly Library, Indiana University, Bloomington, Indiana

Crossing over the Ohio River to Bridgeport, Ohio, he also sketched a hillside landscape scene.

2.18 *Nr. Bridgeport, Ohio*, wash on paper, 1859, 4½ x 7½ in. Courtesy, The Lilly Library, Indiana University, Bloomington, Indiana

Other sketches highlighted buildings near Wheeling including a mill, a local church, and the local poor house.

2.19 *Mill, near Wheeling, Va., October 1859,* wash on paper, 1859, 4½ x 7½ in. Courtesy, The Lilly Library, Indiana University, Bloomington, Indiana

2.20 *Nr. Wheeling, Va. October 1859,* wash on paper, 1859, 4½ x 7½ in. Courtesy, The Lilly Library, Indiana University, Bloomington, Indiana

2.21 *Poor House, Wheeling October 1859*, wash on paper, 1859, 4½ x 7½ in. Courtesy, The Lilly Library, Indiana University, Bloomington, Indiana

Cranstone began November 1859 sketching a distant view of Wheeling from the south showing the city's suspension bridge, which at the time was the longest in the world.   Spanning a branch of the Ohio River to Wheeling Island, the bridge was part of the National Road that continued over a second branch of the river to Bridgeport, Ohio.

2.22 *Wheeling, from Ohio November 1859*, wash on paper, 1859, 4½ x 7½ in. Courtesy, The Lilly Library, Indiana University, Bloomington, Indiana

Lefevre captured the rural nature of the Ohio side of the river outside Bridgeport in a series of eleven sketches. In addition to landscapes, Cranstone's images include several small cabins as well as a dam site.

2.23 *Ohio, November 1859*, wash on paper, 1859, 4½ x 7½ in., Courtesy, The Lilly Library, Indiana University, Bloomington, Indiana

2.24 *Nr. Ohio, November 1859,* wash on paper, 1859, 4½ x 7½ in. Courtesy, The Lilly Library, Indiana University, Bloomington, Indiana

2.25 *Ohio, November 1859*, wash on paper, 1859, 4½ x 7½ in. Courtesy, The Lilly Library, Indiana University, Bloomington, Indiana

Shortly after returning from Ohio, Cranstone left Wheeling traveling by riverboat to Parkersburg, West Virginia. His brother Alfred, likely the young man with the goatee standing on the boat near the gangplank, accompanied Lefevre. The riverboat, depicted below, displays a banner reading "PARKERSBURG AT 10 AM."

2.26 *At the Wharf, Wheeling, Virginia*, wash on paper, 1859, 4½ x 7½ in. Courtesy, The Lilly Library, Indiana University, Bloomington, Indiana

The drawing of another riverboat passing under the Wheeling suspension bridge was prepared about the same time.

2.27 *Suspension Bridge, Ohio River, Wheeling, Virginia*, wash on paper, 1859, 4½ x 7½ in. Courtesy, The Lilly Library, Indiana University, Bloomington, Indiana

While only in Parkersburg a short time, Cranstone still found time to prepare seven sketches of this small, rural town. They include a number of churches that may reflect the artist's strong religious beliefs as well as his interest in sketching buildings with clean, well-defined architectural lines. From Parkersburg, Cranstone continued his journey by riverboat to Cincinnati, Ohio, and then overland to Richmond, Indiana.

2.28 *Parkersburg, Va., November 1859*, wash on paper, 1859, 4½ x 7½ in, Courtesy, The Lilly Library, Indiana University, Bloomington, Indiana

2.29 *Parkersburg, Virginia, November 1859*, wash on paper, 1859, 4½ x 7½ in. Courtesy, The Lilly Library, Indiana University, Bloomington, Indiana

Visit to Richmond, Indiana

Cranstone visited Richmond where a cousin on his mother's side, William M. Lefevre, Jr., resided. According to his great-granddaughter, Mrs. J. Rollins, the former Gertrude Lefevre of Richmond, Indiana, William M. Lefevre, Jr. was the nephew of Cranstone's mother, Maria Lefevre Cranstone.[18] Maria and her brother William were descendents of a Huguenot family that immigrated to England from France about the time of the revocation of the Edict of Nantes in 1685. William moved from England to Utica, New York sometime after his son William Jr.'s birth in 1818. Later, as an adult, William, Jr. met and married, Rebecca Smythe, who was visiting Utica, New York from England. They had three children, Frederick (born 1844), Albert (born 1846), and Ellen (born c.1847).

Lefevres.   Richmond U.S.A.

2.30 *Frederick, Ellen and Albert Lefevre*, Richmond, Indiana, c. 1860, photograph, D/ECe/F-138. Courtesy, Hertfordshire Archives & Local Studies, Hertford, England

About 1857, William M. Lefevre, Jr. moved his family to Richmond, Indiana, where he established the City Stove Store at 70 Main Street. The family resided at 32 North Sixth Street at the southeast corner of North Sixth and Mulberry Streets.[19] During his visit, Cranstone sketched this house with a man, possibly his uncle, standing on the sidewalk. William Lefevre, Jr. died in Richmond at age forty-four of stomach cancer on December 3, 1862.[20]

2.31 *Richmond, Indiana*, wash on paper, 1859, 4½ x 7½ in. Courtesy, The Lilly Library, Indiana University, Bloomington, Indiana

During his stay from early December 1859 to early January 1860, Cranstone made thirty-five sketches of Richmond and its suburbs. One of his earliest sketches depicts the Hicksite meeting house used by local Quakers.

2.32 *Richmond, Indiana, Hicksite Meeting House, December 2nd 1859*, wash on paper, 1859, 4½ x 7½ in. Courtesy, The Lilly Library, Indiana University, Bloomington, Indiana

In contrast to his Wheeling rural sketches of landscapes, his Richmond views were, for the most part, detailed scenes of buildings and everyday life in the business and residential sections of the town. Included were scenes of Main Street, the Citizens Bank operated by Morrisson, Blanchard and Co. on the corner of Main and Fifth Streets with the old City Hall in the background, and the Public School.

2.33 *Richmond, Indiana, Main Street*, wash on paper, 1859, 4½ x 7½ in. Courtesy, The Lilly Library, Indiana University, Bloomington, Indiana

2.34 *Richmond, Indiana,* wash on paper, 1859, 4½ x 7½ in. Courtesy, The Lilly Library, Indiana University, Bloomington, Indiana

2.35 *Richmond, Indiana, Public School*, wash on paper, 1859, 4½ x 7½ in. Courtesy, The Lilly Library, Indiana University, Bloomington, Indiana

The well-groomed mansions of Richmond's prominent citizens on North Seventh and Eighth Streets are also represented in drawings of this part of town. These sketches of urban activities in a bustling Mid-western town showcase Cranstone's talent for drawing buildings, modes of transportation, animals, and people.

2.36 *Richmond, Indiana*, wash on paper, 1859, 4½ x 7½ in. Courtesy, The Lilly Library, Indiana University, Bloomington, Indiana

2.37 *Richmond, Indiana, Seventh Street*, wash on paper, 1859, 4½ x 7½ in. Courtesy, The Lilly Library, Indiana University, Bloomington, Indiana

Cranstone also explored Richmond's outskirts as well. His sketches of the first wooden covered railroad bridge passing over the Whitewater River highlight the bridge's form. Other scenes show men cutting ice and skaters on the frozen river.

2.38 *Richmond, Indiana*, wash on paper, 1859, 4½ x 7½ in. Courtesy, The Lilly Library, Indiana University, Bloomington, Indiana

2.39 *Near Richmond, Indiana, January 2nd. 1860*, wash on paper, 1860, 4½ x 7½ in. Courtesy, The Lilly Library, Indiana University, Bloomington, Indiana

2.40 *Nr. Richmond, Indiana. January 3rd[d] 1860*, wash on paper, 1860, 4½ x 7½ in. Courtesy, The Lilly Library, Indiana University, Bloomington, Indiana

Views of St. Paul's Episcopal Church, the United Presbyterian Church, and the Pearl Street Methodist Episcopal Church once again illustrate Cranstone's inclination to highlight houses of worship.

2.41 *Richmond, Indiana, Episcopal Church*, wash on paper, 1860, 4½ x 7½ in.
Courtesy, The Lilly Library, Indiana University, Bloomington, Indiana

2.42 *Richmond, Indiana,* wash on paper, 1860, 4½ x 7½ in. Courtesy, The Lilly Library, Indiana University, Bloomington, Indiana

2.43 *Richmond, Indiana, Presbyterian Church,* wash on paper, 1860, 4½ x 7½ in. Courtesy, The Lilly Library, Indiana University, Bloomington, Indiana

Cranstone's drawings of Richmond became well known there through a series of articles in the local newspapers. Information about the Comstock family's effort to purchase a portion of the collection interested local readers in 1928.[21] In 1947 the *Palladium-Item and Sun-Telegram* carried a four-part series about the Indiana University Library Cranstone collection.[22] Subsequently in 1951, there was a ten-part series on the artist, his family, and his connection to the William M. Lefevre, Jr., family.[23]

Cranstone's life and art have continued to be featured in additional articles published locally over the years. Images of many of the thirty-five Richmond drawings annotated with the names of buildings including former and present street names were included with the articles. A 1994 article announced the acquisition of the 6 x 12 3/8 in. watercolor by Cranstone titled *Cutting Ice, Near Richmond, Indiana* by the Richmond Art Museum where this beautiful painting hangs today.[24]

Back Through Wheeling

Cranstone left Richmond, Indiana in early January 1860 for points farther east. In Cincinnati, Ohio, on January 10, 1860, he rendered several sketches of the riverfront. Cranstone also crossed to the other side to sketch Covington and Newport, Kentucky.

2.44 *Covington, Kentucky. January 1860,* wash on paper, 1860, 4½ x 7½ in. Courtesy, The Lilly Library, Indiana University, Bloomington, Indiana

2.45 *Newport, Kentucky. January 10ᵗʰ 1860*, wash on paper, 1860, 4½ x 7½ in. Courtesy, The Lilly Library, Indiana University, Bloomington, Indiana

Cranstone either prepared very few drawings during the rest of January and most of February 1860 or they were not included in the collection when it was sold. After leaving Cincinnati he likely took a riverboat back to Wheeling where he spent much of this two-month period. His drawings do not allow for a more definite explanation of where or what he did during this period. He and Alfred possibly stayed with Asa Partridge again. The Lilly Library collection does contain three sketches Cranstone completed near Wheeling dated February 1860 that show houses and outbuildings in hilly, rural areas but do not provide other clues.

Visit to Washington, D. C.

March 1860 found Cranstone in Washington, D. C. where he prepared fourteen sketches that include the Potomac River and a number of detailed views of the capitol's monuments and federal buildings. His finished view of the rear of *The President's House* is now in the White House art collection and was selected by President Carter to be the official White House Christmas card in 1979.[25]

2.46 *The President's House, Washington. March 1860,* wash on paper, 1860, 4½ x 7½ in. Courtesy, The Lilly Library, Indiana University, Bloomington, Indiana

A view of the partially completed Washington Monument and two sketches of the capitol building under construction provide a glimpse of a city's skyline in transition.

2.47 *Washington March, 1860,* wash on paper, 1860, 4½ x 7½ in. Courtesy, The Lilly Library, Indiana University, Bloomington, Indiana

2.48 *Washington*, wash on paper, 1860, 4½ x 7½ in. Courtesy, The Lilly Library, Indiana University, Bloomington, Indiana

2.49 *Washington*, wash on paper, 1860, 4½ x 7½ in., Courtesy, The Lilly Library, Indiana University, Bloomington, Indiana

During a visit to the capitol building he made sketches of two famous statues. The statue labeled *Civilization* by Cranstone is the work of the American sculptor, Horatio Greenough, who called it *Rescue.* Carved while Greenough lived in Florence, Italy, it was installed at the capitol in 1851. The second statue Cranstone titled *Columbus* was sculpted in Naples, Italy by the Italian sculptor, Luigi Persico and first displayed at the capitol building in 1844. Both statues were removed and placed in storage at the Smithsonian Institution in Washington, D.C. in 1958.

2.50   *Civilization by Greenough, at the Capitol, Washington*, wash on paper, 1860, 4½ x 7½ in. Courtesy, The Lilly Library, Indiana University, Bloomington, Indiana

2.51 *Columbus by Persico at the Capitol, Washington*, wash on paper, 1860, 4½ x 7½ in. Courtesy, The Lilly Library, Indiana University, Bloomington, Indiana

Sketches of the City Hall, Treasury Department, Post Office building, and the Patent Office continue to demonstrate Cranstone's artistic and drafting talents. These detailed sketches demonstrate his attention to detail and an understanding of perspective, classical design and shadow no doubt gained during his studies at the Royal Academy of Art in London.

2.52 *Washington, City Hall*, wash on paper, 1860, 4½ x 7½ in. Courtesy, The Lilly Library, Indiana University, Bloomington, Indiana

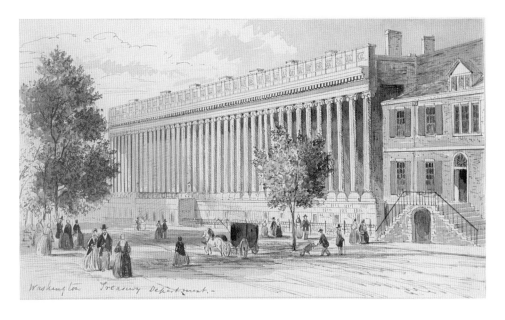

2.53 *Washington Treasury Department*, wash on paper, 1860, 4½ x 7½ in. Courtesy, The Lilly Library, Indiana University, Bloomington, Indiana

2.54 *Washington, Post Office*, wash on paper, 1860, 4½ x 7½ in. Courtesy, The Lilly Library, Indiana University, Bloomington, Indiana

2.55 *Washington, Patent Office*, wash on paper, 1860, 4½ x 7½ in. Courtesy, The Lilly Library, Indiana University, Bloomington, Indiana

Richmond, Virginia and the James River

Cranstone's next stop was Richmond, Virginia, some 106 miles south of Washington. Here, Cranstone prepared sixteen sketches. They include the statehouse, resplendent with the stars and stripes flying overhead, and the nearby Washington Monument with an equestrian statue of George Washington on a star-shaped granite base accompanied by smaller statues of Patrick Henry, George Mason, Thomas Jefferson, and John Marshall. These bronze figures were modeled by Crawford and cast by the Royal foundry in Munich, Germany.[26]

2.56 *State House, Richmond, Virginia,* wash on paper, 1860, 4½ x 7½ in. Courtesy, The Lilly Library, Indiana University, Bloomington, Indiana

2.57 *Monument to Washington, Richmond, Virginia*, wash on paper, 1860, 4½ x 7½ in. Courtesy, The Lilly Library, Indiana University, Bloomington, Indiana

Richmond is located at the point where the terrain transitions from the hilly Piedmont to the flatter Tidewater area. The James River links these two areas as it flows east through the falls at Richmond to the Chesapeake Bay. During a visit to Richmond's western suburbs, Cranstone followed the barge canal that parallels the river, sketching several views.[27] On his return, he sketched the distant city and the bridge of the Richmond and Petersburg rail line crossing the river.

2.58 *James River & Canal, Richmond, Virginia,* wash on paper, 1860, 4½ x 7½ in. Courtesy, The Lilly Library, Indiana University, Bloomington, Indiana

2.59 *Richmond, Virginia,* wash on paper, 1860, 4½ x 7½ in. Courtesy, The Lilly Library, Indiana University, Bloomington, Indiana

From a point known as Church Hill on the east side of Richmond he sketched tobacco warehouses along the river and the statehouse with its flags in the distance. Church Hill derived its name as the site of a number of churches including St. John's Episcopal Church, erected in 1741, the oldest in Richmond. St. John's is where Patrick Henry at the Second Virginia Convention on March 23, 1775 delivered his famous "Give me liberty or give me death" speech in favor of opposing the tyranny of King George III.[28] Cranstone's sketch of the church and its cemetery surrounded by a brick wall depicts a scene quite similar to what exists today on the site.

2.60 *Richmond, Virginia,* wash on paper, 1860, 4½ x 7½ in. Courtesy, The Lilly Library, Indiana University, Bloomington, Indiana

2.61 *St. John's Church, Richmond, Virginia,* wash on paper, 1860, 4½ x 7½ in.
Courtesy, The Lilly Library, Indiana University, Bloomington, Indiana

Cranstone also sketched the James River below the falls where it widens before flowing through Charles City and James City Counties to the Chesapeake Bay. The river is navigable at this point and the sketches show several steam and sail-driven ships docked long the shore.

2.62 *James River, nr. Richmond,* wash on paper, 1860, 4½ x 7½ in. Courtesy, The Lilly Library, Indiana University, Bloomington, Indiana

The York River, Williamsburg and Bigler's Mill

It was now well into March when Cranstone continued east, probably traveling by train the short distance from Richmond to the small town of West Point, Virginia at the head of the York River. Here, he sketched one of the steamboats headed down the York River on its way to Baltimore. His destination, however, was Bigler's Mill, a small lumber mill town just a short way downriver on the south bank of the York River not too distant from Williamsburg.

2.63 *West Point, York River,* wash on paper, 1860, 4½ x 7½ in. Courtesy, The Lilly Library, Indiana University, Bloomington, Indiana

Here, Cranstone and his brother visited their cousin, also named Alfred Cranstone, who lived on a farm not too distant from the wharf at Bigler's Mill.

Alfred B. Cranstone was the only child of James Cranstone, the older brother of Lefevre's father, Joseph Cranstone. Alfred is not a stranger in this story, as it was with Alfred B. and George Cranstone that Lefevre lived in London from 1847 to 1848 as will be discussed in a later chapter. A practicing Quaker, Alfred arrived in America about 1850. He settled in Hanover County just north of Richmond where he was a member of the Quaker Cedar Creek Monthly Meeting. There, he met Hannah Nainly, whose family came from near Williamsburg. Shortly after marrying in 1851 they returned to Hemel Hempstead, England where their first son, Charles, was born.[29] They returned to Hanover County about a year later where their second and third sons, Alfred Henry and William, were born. Sometime after mid 1859, they relocated to a farm near Bigler's Mill, which was part of the plantation known as Ripon Hall established in 1687 by Edmund Jenings.

In addition to being a tenant farmer, Alfred may also have run a gristmill located on nearby Carter's Creek. During the Civil War, Alfred and his family relocated to Westchester County, New York. Returning to Virginia around 1870, Alfred acquired Bush's gristmill close to the Chickahominy River near the small town of Toano about fifteen miles west of Williamsburg.[30]

Lefevre and his brother stayed with their cousin until the end of April and during this time he prepared forty-seven sketches of the Bigler's Mill and Williamsburg area. His watercolors offer interesting views of antebellum Tidewater Virginia, specifically York County and Williamsburg, which had become a declining agricultural area following the move of the state capital from Williamsburg to Richmond in 1780.

Cranstone prepared a number of sketches of the small farms dotting the area including several log cabins that appear to be slave quarters. These sketches offer a unique view of the small homesteads that populated this area of rural Virginia at the time.

2.64 *Near Williamsburg, Virginia,* wash on paper, 1860, 4½ x 7½ in. Courtesy, The Lilly Library, Indiana University, Bloomington, Indiana

2.65 *Near Williamsburg, Virginia,* wash on paper, 1860, 4½ x 7½ in. Courtesy, The Lilly Library, Indiana University, Bloomington, Indiana

2.66 *Near Bigler's Mills, Virginia. March 1860,* wash on paper, 1860, 4½ x 7½ in. Courtesy, The Lilly Library, Indiana University, Bloomington, Indiana

2.67 Near Bigler's Mills, Virginia, wash on paper, 1860, 4½ x 7½ in.
Courtesy, The Lilly Library, Indiana University, Bloomington, Indiana

The Ripon Hall (spelled Rippon by Cranstone) sketches are of a recently built house on the plantation originally settled in the seventeenth century by a well known colonial era official, Edmund Jenings. He became a member of the Council of Virginia in 1691 and was acting governor of the Colony of Virginia from 1706 to 1710. The house, a few miles from Williamsburg, enjoyed a beautiful view from its location on the southern bank of the York River.

2.68 *Rippon Hall, Virginia,* wash on paper, 1860, 4½ x 7½ in. Courtesy, The Lilly Library, Indiana University, Bloomington, Indiana

2.69 *Rippon Hall, Nr. Williamsburg, Virginia,* wash on paper, 1860, 4½ x 7½ in. Courtesy, The Lilly Library, Indiana University, Bloomington, Indiana

Not far from Ripon Hall on the York River was the small community of Bigler's Mill. Mr. James Bigler of Newburgh, New York developed the town in the mid 1850s as a lumber mill and home for its workers.

2.70 *York River, Virginia,* wash on paper, 1860, 4½ x 7½ in. Courtesy, The Lilly Library, Indiana University, Bloomington, Indiana

2.71 *Bigler's Mills, Virginia,* wash on paper, 1860, 4½ x 7½ in. Courtesy, The Lilly Library, Indiana University, Bloomington, Indiana

2.72 *Bigler's Mills, York River, Virginia,* wash on paper, 1860, 4½ x 7½ in. Courtesy, The Lilly Library, Indiana University, Bloomington, Indiana

Cranstone also sketched views of nearby historic Porto Bello, the country retreat of the last royal governor of Virginia, John Murray, Earl of Dunmore, who fled Williamsburg June 8, 1775 on the eve of the American Revolution. Situated on the north bank of Queens Creek just outside Williamsburg, Porto Bello was used by Dunmore to entertain many leading dignitaries of the time, including George Washington. [31]

Porto Bello Virginia: formerly the residence of Lord Dunmore.

2.73 *Porto Bello, Virginia, formerly the residence of Lord Dunmore,* wash on paper, 1860, 4½ x 7½ in. Courtesy, The Lilly Library, Indiana University, Bloomington, Indiana

Cranstone's views of some of Williamsburg's buildings dating from the colonial period provide an interesting snapshot of this quiet village in 1860. Bruton Parish Church on Duke of Gloucester Street (labeled the Episcopal Church in his sketch) was completed in 1715 and its distinctive wooden tower added in 1769.[32] It appears today much as it did in Cranstone's 1860 sketch. Behind the Courthouse, where the Declaration of Independence was read from its steps on July 26, 1776, is the residence of Peyton Randolph, president of the first Continental Congress in Philadelphia. The Powder Magazine, located across the Duke of Gloucester Street from the Courthouse, was built in 1715.

2.74 *Episcopal Church, Williamsburg, Virginia,* wash on paper, 1860, 4½ x 7½ in. Courtesy, The Lilly Library, Indiana University, Bloomington, Indiana

2.75 *Court House, Williamsburg, Virginia March 1860,* wash on paper, 1860, 4½ x 7½ in. Courtesy, The Lilly Library, Indiana University, Bloomington, Indiana

2.76 *Williamsburg, Virginia March 1860,* wash on paper, 1860, 4½ x 7½ in. Courtesy, The Lilly Library, Indiana University, Bloomington, Indiana

The next sketch, known as the Gothic building, stood on the grounds of the first public facility in America to treat the mentally ill. The hospital was opened in 1773 and is still in operation today at a different location in the Williamsburg area.

2.77 *Insane asylum, Williamsburg, Virginia,* wash on paper, 1860, 4½ x 7½ in. Courtesy, The Lilly Library, Indiana University, Bloomington, Indiana

The sketch titled *The Old Palace, Williamsburg, Virginia* depicts the last remaining section of the original Colonial era Governor's Palace at the time of his visit. It had been converted into a private residence that was destroyed during the Civil War.

2.78 *The Old Palace, Williamsburg, Virginia,* wash on paper, 1860, 4½ x 7½ in., Courtesy, The Lilly Library, Indiana University, Bloomington, Indiana

Completing his views of Williamsburg, Cranstone prepared two sketches of the College of William and Mary, the second oldest college in America. Illustrated here is the President's House adjacent to the Wren Building.

2.79 *William and Mary College, Williamsburg, Virginia,* wash on paper, 1860, 4½ x 7½ in, Courtesy, The Lilly Library, Indiana University, Bloomington, Indiana

Harper's Ferry and Back To Wheeling Again

At the end of April 1860, the Cranstone brothers started traveling west again. Their first stop was Harper's Ferry, West Virginia (in the state of Virginia at the time), where Cranstone prepared eight sketches. The town was well known as the site of John Brown's raid on October 16, 1859. Cranstone was well aware of the raid since he was in Wheeling at the time when first news of the raid was carried there by travelers and crews of trains arriving from Harper's Ferry. The local newspaper, the *Wheeling Intelligencer,* printed detailed reports of the raid. Cranstone's anti-slavery views and the participation of Quakers in the raid no doubt caused him to follow the stories carefully.[33]

One sketch Cranstone made from across the Potomac River provides a panoramic view of the town including the buildings that constituted the arsenal involved in the raid. Rendered from a point high on the hill above Harper's Ferry, another sketch shows several church steeples with the Potomac

River in the background. This sketch served as the model for one of the oil paintings Cranstone prepared after his return to England. Other sketches depict barges along the towpath of the Chesapeake and Ohio Canal that runs from Cumberland, Maryland, to Washington, D.C. Thus, while earlier artists had journeyed to Harper's Ferry solely to capture its natural beauty, Cranstone's sketches had the added advantage of bringing to England a more recent view of the town where John Brown's history-making raid had occurred.

2.80 *Harper's Ferry, Virginia,* wash on paper, 1860, 4½ x 7½ in. Courtesy, The Lilly Library, Indiana University, Bloomington, Indiana

2.81 *Harper's Ferry, Virginia,* wash on paper, 1860, 4½ x 7½ in. Courtesy, The Lilly Library, Indiana University, Bloomington, Indiana

2.82 *Harper's Ferry, Virginia,* wash on paper, 1860, 4½ x 7½ in. Courtesy, The Lilly Library, Indiana University, Bloomington, Indiana

Continuing on by train, Cranstone arrived back in Wheeling. During the early part of his third stay in the area, he sketched thirteen views of the Ohio River from a hillside above the riverside town of Warwood just north of Wheeling. These drawings include several of Wheeling and its suspension bridge, the Ohio, and the Twin Sisters Islands just upriver.

2.83 *Wheeling, Virginia,* wash on paper, 1860, 4½ x 7½ in. Courtesy, The Lilly Library, Indiana University, Bloomington, Indiana

2.84 *Ohio River, Wheeling,* wash on paper, 1860, 4½ x 7½ in. Courtesy, The Lilly Library, Indiana University, Bloomington, Indiana

Cranstone revisited familiar sites near Wheeling and sketched the "Indian Cave" located above the entrance of the Hempfield train tunnel near the viaduct. The area along Wheeling Creek drew his attention again, and three sketches were made in the suburb of Elm Grove where they depict one of the stone bridges over the creek, the Shepherd house, and one of the tollhouses from the earlier days of the National Road. Cranstone also prepared two double-page panoramas of Wheeling Creek during this visit.

2:85 *Near Wheeling, Virginia,* wash on paper, 1860, 4½ x 7½ in. Courtesy, The Lilly Library, Indiana University, Bloomington, Indiana

2.86 *Wheeling Creek, Virginia,* wash on paper, 1860, 4½ x 7½ in. Courtesy, The Lilly Library, Indiana University, Bloomington, Indiana

2.87 *Nr. Wheeling, Virginia,* wash on paper, 1860, 4½ x 7½ in. Courtesy, The Lilly Library, Indiana University, Bloomington, Indiana

Before leaving the Wheeling area, Cranstone visited the Ohio countryside again. Here, he sketched a farmstead near the small town of Bridgeport and four sketches depicting the creek running next to the road to Clairsville, Ohio.

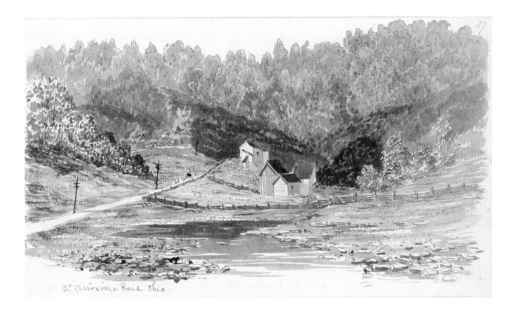

2.88 *St. Clairsville Road Ohio,* wash on paper, 1860, 4½ x 7½ in. Courtesy, The Lilly Library, Indiana University, Bloomington, Indiana

The Cranstones departed Wheeling for the last time in June 1860 traveling north along the Ohio River. Several more views of the river from its banks were done at this time. A striking view of a steamboat with the sun bursting through the clouds is the last sketch he made of the Ohio River.

2.89 *Ohio River,* wash on paper, 1860, 4½ x 7½ in. Courtesy, The Lilly Library, Indiana University, Bloomington, Indiana

Upon reaching Wellsville, Ohio, about fifty miles north of Wheeling, Cranstone drew four sketches of the small river town and the railroad line serving it. While waiting for the train to Cleveland, he sketched a cartoon showing three men, feet up on the walls and table, with the notice "Gentlemen are requested not to STEAL THE PAPERS." The drawing is most likely a self-portrait of the artist on the right, his younger brother Alfred on the left, and an unidentified traveler in the center.

2.90 *Do not steal the papers,* wash on paper, 1860, 4½ x 7½ in. Courtesy, The Lilly Library, Indiana University, Bloomington, Indiana

Cleveland, Ohio and Buffalo, New York

After arriving in Cleveland, Cranstone made a single sketch showing a wide, tree-lined street with several buildings, church towers reaching to the sky, and elegantly dressed residents promenading on foot and in horse-driven carriages. He then continued most likely by steamer on Lake Erie to Buffalo, New York where one of his three sketches shows the steamer *City of Buffalo* at a dock with commercial buildings in the background. Two other sketches of the harbor area suggest the location is near the western terminus for the Erie Canal. A canal boat being pulled by a horse appears in one view, while the other includes a portion of the canal and a large building with the name "Frontier Mills" on its side.

2.91 *Cleveland, Ohio*, wash on paper, 1860, 4½ x 7½ in. Courtesy, The Lilly Library, Indiana University, Bloomington, Indiana

2.92 *Buffalo*, wash on paper, 1860, 4½ x 7½ in. Courtesy, The Lilly Library, Indiana University, Bloomington, Indiana

2.93 *Buffalo,* wash on paper, 1860, 4½ x 7½ in, Courtesy, The Lilly Library, Indiana University, Bloomington, Indiana

2.94 *Buffalo,* wash on paper, 1860, 4½ x 7½ in. Courtesy, The Lilly Library, Indiana University, Bloomington, Indiana

American and Canadian Views of Niagara Falls

From Buffalo, Cranstone proceeded to Niagara Falls to sketch thirty drawings of this natural wonder of the world, including ten double-page panoramic scenes. No doubt the sound of the falls first caught his attention when he stopped at Chippewa, some three miles upstream from the actual falls, to prepare his first sketches.   He then followed the river downstream, preparing additional sketches as the water rushed past Goat Island and under a bridge connecting it and the mainland.

2.95 *Falls of Niagara-From Chippewa 3 miles,* wash on paper, 1860, 4½ x 7½ in. Courtesy, The Lilly Library, Indiana University, Bloomington, Indiana

2.96 *Niagara,* wash on paper, 1860, 4½ x 7½ in. Courtesy, The Lilly Library, Indiana University, Bloomington, Indiana

2.97 *The Falls of Niagara, The American Falls,* wash on paper, 1860, 4 ½ x 7½ in. Courtesy, The Lilly Library, Indiana University, Bloomington, Indiana

With the American falls in the background, Cranstone recorded a sign recalling a visitor who lost her life: "This is the spot where Miss Martha K. Rugg lost her life by falling over THE PRECIPICE 167 ft. while plucking a flower, August 24ᵗʰ, 1844."

2.98 *At the Falls of Niagara,* wash on paper, 1860, 4½ x 7½ in. Courtesy, The Lilly Library, Indiana University, Bloomington, Indiana

Several sketches are reminders that in 1860, Niagara Falls was already a tourist destination. The sign on a small building next to the rapids on the American side reads: "Refreshments and Rock Ornaments," while a sketch of another building not shown is identified as "The Old Curiosity Shop."

2.99 *Falls of Niagara – The Rapids,* wash on paper, 1860, 4½ x 7½ in. Courtesy, The Lilly Library, Indiana University, Bloomington, Indiana

While most of his sketches of the falls were done from the Canadian side, there is one spectacular view of both falls made from the American side. In the follow-on sketch, he captured the enormous power of the Canadian falls and the enclosed stairway used to access an observation portal at its base.

2.100 *Falls of Niagara,* wash on paper, 1860, 4½ x 7½ in. Courtesy, The Lilly Library, Indiana University, Bloomington, Indiana

2.101 *Falls of Niagara,* wash on paper, 1860, 4½ x 7½ in. Courtesy, The Lilly Library, Indiana University, Bloomington, Indiana

Cranstone's sketches of the suspension bridge crossing the Niagara River gorge and the towns on the American and Canadian sides provide a glimpse of their appearance during this period.

2.102 *Suspension Bridge Niagara,* wash on paper, 1860, 4 ½ x 7½ in. Courtesy, The Lilly Library, Indiana University, Bloomington, Indiana

2.103 *Falls of Niagara. Canada side,* wash on paper, 1860, 4½ x 7½ in. Courtesy, The Lilly Library, Indiana University, Bloomington, Indiana

2.104 *Niagara,* wash on paper, 1860, 4½ x 7½ in. Courtesy, The Lilly Library, Indiana University, Bloomington, Indiana

New York City and the Trip Home

From Niagara Falls, Cranstone continued to New York City. On the way, did he possibly stop in Utica, New York, the first place his Lefevre relatives lived after they arrived in the United States? Even though this possibility had been hinted at in the notes left by his nephew Arthur Cranstone, it seems unlikely he stopped there since there is no evidence from his sketches that he visited Utica either during the early portion or this later stage of his trip.

Cranstone made only a few sketches in New York City as he waited to depart for England. One depicts a tower-like building topped with a weather vane. Cranstone originally labeled this drawing *Evergreen Cemetery, Brooklyn, Long Island* but later crossed out "Evergreen" and replaced it with "Greenwood," the name of another well-known cemetery in Brooklyn. However, comparison of the structure depicted in the sketch with current photographs of the cemeteries confirms Evergreen Cemetery as the correct location. The Evergreen Cemetery, established in 1847, is located on the border between Brooklyn and Queens and is the final resting place for nearly 519,000 persons, including a number of historic personages.[34] Possibly a relative or family friend may be buried at the cemetery, but it is not possible to search for anyone interred there prior to 1942 without knowing the date of burial.

2.105 *Greenwood Cemetery, Brooklyn, Long Island,* wash on paper, 1860, 4½ x 7½ in. Courtesy, The Lilly Library, Indiana University, Bloomington, Indiana

While waiting to board the ship *Vigo*[35] at the lower end of Manhattan Island, Cranstone sketched what is most likely a distant view of the East Battery on Governor's Island, one of five forts built to protect New York harbor from a possible British attack during the War of 1812. He ended his collection of American views with a detailed sketch of the Castle Garden Depot, the former Fort Clinton, also built in 1812 and known as the West Battery. It served as the primary immigration center for the United States between 1850 and 1890 until the establishment of Ellis Island in 1892. This site, now known as Battery Park, is the point where ferries and tour boats depart for the Statue of Liberty and Ellis Island.[36]

2.106 *Castle Garden Depot, New York,* wash on paper, 1860, 4½ x 7½ in. Courtesy, The Lilly Library, Indiana University, Bloomington, Indiana

Cranstone left the United States on June 22, 1860 from Castle Garden, the same place he had landed a little over nine months earlier. He and Alfred traveled in steerage during the return journey as depicted in several sketches. The *Vigo* put into Queenstown, Ireland, during the return voyage and Cranstone's last sketch is a panoramic double-page view of this town, as the ship passed that point.

2.107 *Off Queenstown, Ireland,* wash on paper, 1860, double panels, 4½ x 15 in. Courtesy, The Lilly Library, Indiana University, Bloomington, Indiana

3

On Slavery

The *Vigo* arrived in Liverpool July 9, 1860 following a twenty-day voyage across the ocean. After clearing customs in Liverpool, Lefevre and Alfred returned to Hemel Hempstead completing their journey to the United States almost ten and one-half months after their departure. Cranstone resumed painting and returned to his position as an art and drawing instructor in his wife's school.

Later in the year, December 29, 1860 to be precise, Cranstone wrote a letter to the editor of the weekly *Hemel Hempstead Gazette* about his trip to America.[37] In the lengthy letter, the only known existing correspondence authored by Cranstone, he expressed his views of the state of America with particular reference to slavery. The letter reveals Cranstone as a well-read man of keen intellect who developed a deep appreciation of the political and social problems of America. It seems clear from reading the letter (the full text of the letter can be found as an Appendix) that his ten-month journey to America was most likely motivated as much by his desire to experience firsthand the evils of slavery as to visit relatives and draw the landscapes so wonderfully captured in his sketches. However, one particularly relevant passage bears repeating now:

> But it is in the slave auction rooms where the horrors of the system are most palpable to the eye. No pen can adequately describe scenes so revolting to the mind of a stranger. It was in the month of March of this present year, that being at Richmond, Virginia, I turned down a back street and saw a row of dirty looking houses to the doors of which were posted red flags on which were pinned pieces of paper announcing the time of sale of the human merchandise within. Entering one of these low dens in company with a motley crowd, the first object that met the eye was a company of coloured women and young girls, seated

on benches awaiting the sale. The men and boys are placed behind a screen at the further end of the room, surrounded by an eager crowd of purchasers, each slave being stripped to the waist, that he may be tested as to soundness and bodily health. The saleroom was long, dark and dingy, with a raised platform on one side for the salesman and the "lot." Awaiting the arrival for the auctioneer, these goods are freely handled and inspected. Here is every shade of complexion from purest ebony to white, black field hands, yellow beauties, stout fellows; if the buyer wishes bright-eyed, smooth of skin, supple of form, full-chested, clean-limbed creatures, culinary prodigies, deft seamstresses, delightful washerwomen, charioteers, unrivalled, the very treasures of commercial Christianity; the only adequate exponents of Virginian wealth and enterprise. The women are dressed in flaunting gay colours, the men in their best trim. The auctioneer arrives, the sale commences. I see one after another mount the platform—the men first, the women and children last. And they are quickly knocked down, showing a brisk demand in the market. Whilst the sale is progressing, each slave is subjected to a close examination; their arms and hands are felt—teeth inspected—made to walk up and down the room, and to mount and remount the platform. In spite of what is so often said in contradiction to the parting of families, I was an eyewitness that such is the fact; several young children and their mothers being knocked down to different purchasers. With a long-drawn breath I follow the crowd out, who made their way to another room, where the same scene is enacted. Day after day these scenes are going on in the midst of churches and chapels, and within a stone's throw of a splendid monument of Washington.

The Painting *Slave Market in America, 1862*

The Washington monument referred to above still stands on the grounds of the State Capitol in Richmond, Virginia. The spot is near Shockoe Bottom where the slave markets Cranstone describes were located. After his return to England, Cranstone painted the oil on fabric *Slave Auction, Virginia,* most likely based on a sketch he prepared that is now lost. It was first exhibited at the Royal Society of British Artists in Suffolk Street, London in 1863.[38] [39] The painting was next seen when auctioned by Christie, Manson and Woods in London on February 17, 1928 for a price of ten pounds, ten shillings to a Mr. Mason.[40] Over sixty years later, the same painting, without attribution, was purchased by a dealer at Sotheby's London on October 24, 1990. Acquired by the Virginia Historical Society, Richmond in 1991, this painting today is prominently displayed in their *The*

Story of Virginia, an American Experience exhibit.

3.1 *Slave Auction, Virginia,* 1863, oil on fabric, 13 x 21 in. Courtesy, Virginia Historical Society, Richmond, Virginia

David Hackett Fischer and James C. Kelly, in their book *Away I'm Bound Away*, state that when the painting was conserved after the 1990 sale, the inscription "Slave Auction Virginia/Painted by I Cranstone/Hemel Hempstead Hert" (Hertfordshire) was found on the frame. While this inscription confirms Cranstone as the artist, his identification with the painting is further solidified by how closely it reproduces the slave auction he described in his letter.

Fischer and Kelly also point out the Cranstone *Slave Auction, Virginia* painting is identical to an oil painting, 13 x 21 in., titled *Richmond Slave Market Auction,* attributed to British artist Eyre Crowe (1824-1910) in the collection of Jay P. Altmayer of Alabama. They questioned whether this painting was the work of Cranstone rather than Crowe. [41]

In considering this question, it is known Cranstone prepared more than one copy of his paintings. A comparison of *Slave Auction, Virginia* to *Richmond Slave Market Auction* shows they are virtually identical with respect to size, subject matter and artistic quality. Minor differences such as *Slave Auction, Virginia* having eighteen ceiling beams and a curtain on the right-hand side window while *Richmond Slave Market Auction* has eight ceiling beams and no curtain on the same window were noted, but they do not detract from the overall conclusion the paintings are by the same artist. Based on the available evidence it is my opinion *Richmond Slave Market and Slave Auction, Virginia* were both painted by Lefevre James Cranstone.[42]

Cranstone's full letter makes other references to slavery, mentioning the abolitionist John Brown's raid at Harper's Ferry and the effect it had on influencing a reign of terror that tightened the chains of the slave. Having been in nearby Wheeling in October 1859 when John Brown's raid occurred, Cranstone took himself to Harper's Ferry only five months after this historic event for a first hand look. After returning to England he painted the 24 x 26 in. oil on canvas of Harper's Ferry titled: *A View of the Town on the Potomac River, West Virginia* based on one of his sketches (Illustration 2.81) in the Lilly Library collection. The painting is a view from the hillside above Harper's Ferry with the Shenandoah River in the background. The painting was offered for sale in London in 1968 and its current whereabouts is unknown.[43]

4

More Watercolor Paintings

Almost five years after the first collection of Cranstone watercolor sketches was offered for sale in 1928, another collection of ninety-eight watercolors based on the earlier sketches was auctioned at Sotheby & Co., London on March 29, 1933. Apparently done at Cranstone's leisure after his return to England, the watercolors are larger, richer in detail, and more complete in the use of coloring than the originals. The owner, T. R. Robinson of 25 Campden Hill Gardens, W.S., London, claimed he found them stored in an attic and knew nothing about the artist.[44]

The new collection is a broad representation of the 296 sketches in the Lilly Library collection. Listed consecutively in the Sotheby auction catalogue under lots 39 through 76 they are as follows: twenty one views of Richmond, Indiana; four of Covington, Kentucky; two of Newport, Kentucky; two of Washington, D.C.; two of Buffalo, N.Y.; one of Long Island, N.Y.; sixteen of Niagara Falls; two of Halifax, Nova Scotia; five of Bridgeport, Ohio; one of Cincinnati, Ohio; one of Benwood, Virginia (now West Virginia); three of Harper's Ferry, Virginia (now West Virginia); four of Parkersburg, Virginia (now West Virginia); five of Richmond, Virginia; twenty eight of the Wheeling, West Virginia area; eight of Williamsburg, Virginia; two of Bigler's Mills, York River, Virginia; and one of Ripon Hall, York River, Virginia.

Because of a lack of interest, all ninety-eight paintings were sold for an aggregate price of less than $600.00, primarily to London dealers. The highest price was $54.00 for a view of the *Market Place, Halifax, Nova Scotia,* while a pair of views of the *College of William and Mary* sold for $43.00. The painting of the *Railway Station in Washington,* D.C. brought $14.00. The remaining ninety-four paintings sold at comparably lower prices.[45]

There still was considerable interest in the watercolors. This time, unlike as described in Chapter One when the 304 Cranstone sketches were available, John D. Rockefeller, Jr. did not let the eight watercolors of Williamsburg being offered slip away. With Rockefeller's concurrence, his aide Colonel Arthur Woods, arranged for lots 71, 72, 73, and 74 to be purchased by art dealer P. & D. Colnaghi & Co. Ltd., London. [46] The price, including the Colnaghi commission, averaged $19.40 per painting. After receipt and inspection by Rockefeller in New York City, the paintings were framed and forwarded for exhibition at Colonial Williamsburg. [47]

4.1 *Court House of 1770,* 1860, watercolor on paper, 7 ¾ x 12 ¾ in. Courtesy, Colonial Williamsburg Foundation

Alexander W. Weddell, the owner of Virginia House, Richmond, Virginia, purchased six Virginia scenes. Mr. Weddell, through B. F. Stevens & Brown, Ltd., acquired lots 58, 61, 62 and 63 consisting of one watercolor of Benwood, Virginia (now West Virginia) and five of Richmond, Virginia. These paintings are now in the collection of the Virginia Historical Society.[48]

In 2000, the Virginia Historical Society received from the estate of Paul Mellon six additional Cranstone paintings originally purchased at the Sotheby's auction depicting, respectively, Richmond, Bigler's Mill, and Rippon Hall, Virginia as well as Harper's Ferry, Bedford, and Wheeling, West Virginia.

4.2 *Richmond, Virginia,* 1860, watercolor on paper, 7 ½ x 11 ¾ in. Courtesy, Virginia Historical Society, Richmond, Virginia

The Virginia Museum of Fine Arts, Richmond had previously received in 1985 three of Cranstone's watercolors as gifts from the Paul Mellon Collection. The watercolors include two views of the York River and another of paddle steamers on the James River just downriver from Richmond.[49]   In the illustration below, the artist Cranstone sketches while sitting on the south shore of the York River near Ripon Hall. The man shown standing behind him is most likely his younger brother Alfred who accompanied him on the trip.

4.3   *York River, Virginia, Biglers Mill – With Artist and a Man Standing Behind Him,* 1860, watercolor on paper, 6 ¼ x 13 in. Courtesy, Virginia Museum of Fine Arts, Richmond. The Paul Mellon Collection

Five Cranstone watercolors of street scenes in Richmond, Indiana[50] are part of the Indiana Historical Society, Indianapolis, Indiana art collection.

4.4 *Richmond, Indiana, Seventh St,* 1860, watercolor on paper, 5 ½ x 13 1/8 in. Courtesy, Indiana Historical Society

In 1961, Mr. Wilmar Lewis from Connecticut donated to the White House two watercolor paintings of the White House and the Washington train station. As mentioned previously, President Jimmy Carter chose one of them, *The President's House, Rear View, 1860,* as the 1979 White House Christmas card.[51]

4.5 *White House, Rear View, 1860,* 1860, watercolor on paper, 7 1/16 x 12 7/16 in. Courtesy, "The White House" (249), Washington, D.C.

Senator John D. Rockefeller IV of West Virginia has five Cranstone watercolors in his personal art collection. They depict scenes of West Virginia including the *Suspension Bridge at Wheeling*, several Wheeling area farmsteads, and a view of a railroad track near Wheeling.[52]

4.6 *Near Wheeling, West Virginia,* 1860, watercolor on paper, 13 ½ x 18 ¾ in. Courtesy, Senator & Mrs. John D. Rockefeller IV Collection

Thirteen Cranstone watercolors owned by the Boston Museum of Fine Arts were a gift from Maxim Karolik and are part of the museum's M. and M. Karolik Collection of American Water Colors, Drawings, and Prints 1800-1875. Eleven are views of Harper's Ferry, Richmond, Indiana, and Wheeling, West Virginia, while another two depict Frontier Mills near the western end of the Erie Canal near Buffalo, New York.[53]

4.7 *Woodland Road in (West) Virginia,* 1859-1860, watercolor on paper, Sheet: 6 9/16 x 11 15/16 in. Courtesy, Museum of Fine Arts, Boston, The M. and M. Karolik Collection of American Watercolors, Drawings, and Prints, 1800-1875, 51.2518. Photograph © 2003 Museum of Fine Arts, Boston

The Oglebay Institute Mansion Museum in Wheeling, West Virginia, possesses six of the watercolors purchased from Kennedy and Co., New York, in 1953. These paintings depicting views of the Ohio River near Wheeling, the Suspension Bridge at Wheeling, Wheeling Creek, and a church near Wheeling were highlighted in a wonderful exhibition of Cranstone's works held by the museum in 1984.[54]

4.8 *Mills Near Wheeling, Virginia,* 1860, watercolor on paper, 6 3/8 x 12 ¼ in. Courtesy, Oglebay Institute Mansion Museum, Wheeling, West Virginia

The Richmond Art Museum, Richmond, Indiana, purchased Cranstone's *View of Cutting Ice* from the Hirsch and Adler Galleries, Inc., New York, in 1994. The museum, the only one in the United States to be housed in a public school, is located in McGuire Memorial hall in the north wing of Richmond High School.[55]

4.9 *View of Cutting Ice,* 1860, watercolor on paper, 6 x 12 3/8 in. Courtesy, Richmond Art Museum, Richmond, Indiana

The Sterling and Francine Clark Art Institute, Williamstown, Massachusetts possesses a Cranstone watercolor depicting a small farmstead in western Virginia (now West Virginia).[56]

A watercolor titled *Near Wheeling* that depicts a scene of Wheeling Creek in the area of Elm Grove to the east of Wheeling is in a private collection in Virginia.

The Cranstone watercolor titled *A View of the Market Place, Halifax* is part of the William Inglis Morse Collection of the Killam Memorial Library at Dalhousie University, Halifax, Nova Scotia. Sterling Clark and William Inglis Morse probably acquired their respective paintings at the time of the 1933 Sotheby's London auction.[57]

The paintings in these collections account for fifty-nine of the ninety-eight watercolors auctioned at Sotheby's London in March 1933. Thirty-nine are still unaccounted-for and no doubt some will be found on walls, in trunks, or in storage rooms in the United States, Canada, Great Britain, and Australia. It is hoped readers will recognize one or more of the unaccounted for paintings and make them available for others to appreciate and admire.

The same Sotheby auction also offered as lot 77 a set of Cranstone's series of etchings from 1849 consisting of a title and thirteen plates with the original portfolio. The etchings did not sell and probably were returned to Mr. T. R. Robinson, the ostensible owner. It is likely that Mr. Robinson was actually an intermediary for Cranstone's nephew, Arthur Cranstone, who had put the earlier sketches up for sale in 1928. A set of fourteen etchings matching the description of those offered at the auction passed down through the family by Arthur Cranstone is now part of the Cranstone art collection on loan to the Dacorum Heritage Trust Ltd in Berkhamsted, England.

5

His Life and Career in England

Lefevre James Cranstone considered himself a professional artist from an early age until his death at age seventy-one. Known primarily for his genre-type landscapes in both oil and watercolor, he also did etchings, pen and ink drawings, cartoons, lithographs and portraits. Cranstone also taught art to students at the boarding school run by his wife. Surprisingly, over six hundred of his works survive and as outlined earlier can be found in private and public collections around the world.

I researched the Cranstone family and learned that in 1798 the artist's grandfather Joseph Cranstone, a Quaker, moved from Horsham, Sussex to Hemel Hempstead, Hertfordshire. Hemel Hempstead, located twenty miles northwest of London, traces its rich history back to the days of the Norman Conquest. There at 25 High Street, Cranstone, along with his wife Sarah nee Pollard, their three sons George, James and Joseph, Jr. and daughter Sarah established a residence and ironmongery business. The presence of a Quaker Meetinghouse and the town's position as a principal corn market for London made it a good place to run a business and raise a family. After Joseph's death in 1811, his wife and eldest son George ran the business until 1818 when Joseph, Jr., who had studied engineering, took it over. He expanded the company by adding an iron foundry. Under the name, Phoenix Works, the company was known for building machinery such as fire engines and agricultural equipment.[58]

5.1 *Portrait of Sarah Pollard Cranstone*, 1841, 11 x 12 ¼ in. oil on fabric. Courtesy, Mrs. Sheila Gander

The younger Joseph married Maria Lefevre of Staines, Middlesex County, on August 17, 1819, at the Longford Monthly Meeting of Friends in Hemel Hempstead. Present at the wedding were her parents, Thomas Lefevre, brassier,[59] and his wife Sarah. The newly married couple's marriage certificate also lists as witnesses the names of Joseph Cranstone's two brothers and sister, other members of the Lefevre and Pollard families, and friends.[60] The Lefevre family descended from French Huguenots who moved to England following the Revocation of the Edict of Nantes in 1685.

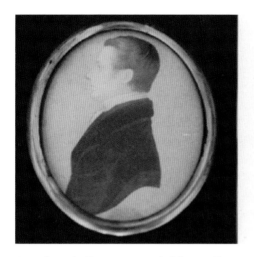 

5.2 *Joseph Cranstone* and *Maria Cranstone,* c. 1840, 3 ¼ x 2 ¾ in., watercolors. Courtesy, Mrs. Sheila Gander

Joseph, Jr. and Maria had fifteen children over a twenty-three year period with the first, George, born June 1, 1820 and the last, Frederick, born August 9, 1843. Three of the children died within a few months of their birth. When he retired in 1863, Joseph, Jr. chose his fourteenth son, William Henry Cranstone, to succeed him in the business. Joseph, Jr., died in Hemel Hempstead on November 22, 1878. Among the structures he built surviving today is the beautiful iron bridge across the River Gade in Gadebridge Park, a drinking fountain erected in 1835 commemorating the 300th anniversary of the first printing of the English Bible, and a water pump outfitted as a street lamp located at the northern end of High Street.[61]

5.3 Gadebridge Park Bridge, Hemel Hempstead, England, 2002, photo. Courtesy, the author

The Royal Academy of Arts Schools, London

Lefevre James Cranstone, their second son, was born March 6, 1822, in Hemel Hempstead. There is no information about Lefevre's early years other than that he resided with his family at 25 High Street. His interest in art appears to have begun at an early age although nothing indicates that relatives on either side of his family had an artistic flair.

This early interest in art was encouraged by his family who enrolled Cranstone about 1838 in Henry Sass's School of Art on Charlotte Street in Bloomsbury, London. Sass's school was well known and many of the art students who subsequently entered the Royal Academy of Arts in this period studied there. Cranstone, with Henry Sass's recommendation, was accepted as a probationer at the coveted Royal Academy Schools as part of a class of twelve students shortly after his eighteenth birthday April 21, 1840.[62]

Probationers were given three months to prepare a set of drawings or models for review by the Council, the ruling body of the Academy. After acceptance, students were formally enrolled in, consecutively, the Antique School, Life School, and the Painting School. When he joined the Royal Academy, students had to finish all three schools within ten years. Unfortunately, no records were kept of a student's progress through the schools or whether he remained for the full term, so it is not known how long Cranstone studied at the Academy.[63] However, based on information in the exhibit catalogs of his early paintings, Cranstone resided in London from the time he enrolled at the Academy until at least 1851.

The earliest known art attributed to Cranstone is a lithograph, 9 3/8 x 3 1/8 in. drawn on stone, titled *Hemel Hempstead from the North East* dated circa 1840 that depicts his hometown of Hemel Hempstead from a nearby hill and surrounding farmland.[64] A copy of this lithograph is in the collection of the Dacorum Heritage Trust Ltd, Berkhamsted.

Cranstone also prepared a watercolor painting of historic St. Mary's church in Hemel Hempstead as seen from nearby Gadebridge Park.

5.4 *St. Mary's Church, Hemel Hempstead*, c. 1840, watercolor on paper, 10 ¼ x 12.0 in. Courtesy, Mrs. Sheila Gander.

Cranstone's first known exhibition took place in 1845 at the Royal Academy when he entered an oil painting titled *A Country Fair*.[65]   *The Lace Maker*, an oil painting, was later shown at the annual exhibition of the Royal Society of British Artists in Suffolk Street, London in 1847 [66] and *Waiting at the Station*, another oil painting, at the Royal Academy in 1850.[67]

5.5 *Waiting at the Station*, 1850, oil on canvas, 26 x 42 in., whereabouts unknown.

Cranstone's addresses in London during the time of these exhibitions were respectively, 5 Cardington Street (1845), 30 New Street, Dorset Square (1847), and 34 Frederick Place, Hampstead Road (1850). While the names of residents at the time for the Cardington Street and Frederick Place addresses were not found, it appears Cranstone stayed with his cousin Alfred B. Cranstone and either his older brother or uncle (both were named George Cranstone), ironmongers, at the 30 New Street, Dorset Square address from 1847 to 1848.[68] It is interesting to note this cousin is the same Alfred B. Cranstone that Lefevre and his brother Alfred stayed with in the Williamsburg area during their visit to Virginia twelve years later.

In 1847, during a trip away from London, Cranstone painted a pair of watercolors of the Swarthmore Quaker Meeting House near Ulverston, Cumbria (formerly Lancashire). The elderly man shown leaving the meetinghouse may very well be Cranstone's grandfather.

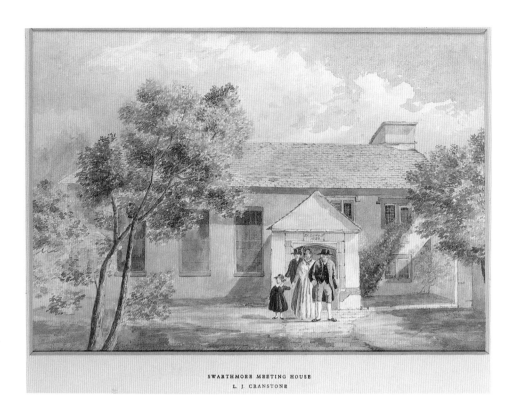

SWARTHMORE MEETING HOUSE
L. J. CRANSTONE

5.6 *Swarthmore Meeting House*, 1847, watercolor, 12 ¼ x 8 ½ in. Courtesy, David Cranstone and Dacorum Heritage Trust Ltd, Berkhamsted, England

Cranstone was in London at the same time two well-known British artists also began their careers and he may have known either one or both. Notes prepared by a family member mention that Lefevre studied art under the well-known British genre artist, William Powell Frith (1819-1909), but no dates or locations were provided to substantiate this claim.[69] It now appears that Cranstone did not study under Frith; rather, the two artists most likely studied at the Royal Academy Schools at the same time. Frith and Dante Gabriel Rossetti, one of the founders of the Pre-Raphaelite Brotherhood, both attended Sass's School of Art, Frith enrolling in 1835 and Rossetti in 1841. Each also attended the Royal Academy Schools, Frith beginning in 1837[70] and Rossetti in 1846[71].

There are a number of similarities between the works of Cranstone and Frith. Given their similar ages and interests in genre type paintings, it is possible they continued any relationship developed in London. Both also painted near the Kent coast with Cranstone known to have painted a series of four undated watercolors (possibly c. 1850) entitled *On the Beach at Margate, Dumpton Gap near Broadstairs, Figures on the Beach at Broadstairs* and *Near*

Broadstairs[72] while Frith attracted further notice with his painting entitled *Ramsgate Sands (Life at the Seaside)* commissioned in 1851 and completed in 1854.[73] It is also of interest that both artists were fond of producing more than one copy of a painting. Another similarity can be seen in Cranstone's *Waiting at the Station* (1850), one of many paintings done of the train station platform during the Victorian era, prepared some twelve years before Frith's *The Railway Station* first exhibited in 1862.[74]

5.7 *Figures on the Beach at Broadstairs*, c.1850, watercolor on paper, 4 ¾ x 7.0 in., whereabouts unknown.

"Fugitive Etchings"

Cranstone did not focus solely on oils and watercolors during this period in London. In 1849, he published a folio of seventeen etchings referred to as "Fugitive Etchings". The British Museum obtained a set in 1878 and examination of these etchings shows they are wonderfully prepared, detailed views of ruins, castles, and everyday scenes in England and Scotland. The cover page titled *ETCHINGS by L. J. CRANSTONE 1849* depicts the remains of the Old Bury House (now known as Charter Tower) in Hemel Hempstead. The *Remains of the Old Bury House, Hemel Hempstead* and the *Clock House - St. Albans* depict scenes from the Hertfordshire area.

5.8 *Remains of the Old Bury House, Hemel Hempstead,* 1849, copper plate engraving, 8.5 x 4.0 in. Courtesy, David Cranstone and Dacorum Heritage Trust Ltd, Berkhamsted, England

5.9 *Clock House, St. Albans*, 1849, copper plate engraving, 6.0 x 5 ½ in. Courtesy, David Cranstone and Dacorum Heritage Trust Ltd, Berkhamsted, England

In the Southampton area, Cranstone etched scenes titled *Landing Oysters near Southampton, Netley Abbey Ruin near Southampton* and *At Redbridge near Southampton.* Similarly, his Plymouth area etchings include *The Quay – Plymouth, Near the Hoe - Plymouth,* and *Milk Boy – a Sketch near Plymouth.* In the Reading area he prepared an etching of the *Gateway at St. Mary's Abbey.*

5.10 *Netley Abbey*, 1849, copper plate engraving, 7.5 x 5 ½ in. Courtesy, David Cranstone and Dacorum Heritage Trust Ltd, Berkhamsted, England

Near the Hoe, Plymouth

5.11 *Near the Hoe, Plymouth,* 1849, copper plate engraving, 7.0 x 5.0 in. Courtesy, David Cranstone and Dacorum Heritage Trust Ltd, Berkhamsted, England

Cranstone included a number of important historic sites in Scotland, such as *Stirling Castle* north of Glasgow, *Roslin Castle* just south of Edinburgh, the *Town and Bridge of Dunkeld* north of Edinburgh and the *Dunkeld Cathedral Ruin.* The set of seventeen etchings also contains scenes titled *John Knox's House, a Cottage Interior, The Ferry Boat* and *The Traveling Tinker.*

5.12 *Cottage Interior,* 1849, copper plate engraving, 6 ½ x 5 ¾ in. Courtesy, David Cranstone and Dacorum Heritage Trust Ltd, Berkhamsted, England

The British Museum also holds a partial second set of eight etchings prepared by Cranstone dated 1854. The title page is identical to that of the first set except for the date 1854 with an imprint showing it was published by J. Hogarth, 5 Haymarket, a prominent publisher at the time. This partial set includes the etchings of *John Knox's House, Stirling Castle, Roslin Castle, the Town and Bridge of Dunkeld, Dunkeld Cathedral Ruin* and two new etchings. The new titles are *The Birth Place of the Poet Rogers* (most likely Newington Green, the birthplace of Samuel Rogers 1763-1855) and *Mr. Roger's House from the Park,* probably a reference to Green Park, London that has a view to the townhouse at 22 St. James Place where Samuel Rogers lived from 1803 until his death.

The quality and dimensions of the imprints of both sets held by the British Museum appear to be identical, suggesting they were prepared from engraved steel plates. It thus seems probable that even though the publisher's name is not present on the frontispiece of the first set (it could have been present on the original folio that held the set which is not included), most likely it was published by J. Hogarth as well.

When the 1849 and 1854 sets were examined, it was noted that a different method of imprinting was used for each set. The 1849 etchings were first printed on tissue paper, cut to a size of 6 1/16 x 9 5/8 inches and adhered to a thicker 11 1/16 x 17.0 in. paper stock. The 1854 set was imprinted directly onto the paper stock leaving a bordered indentation of 6 1/16 x 9 7/8 in. Further, the total of twenty-one different subjects found between the two sets suggests that other editions may have been published between 1849 and 1854.

A third partial set of fourteen etchings dated 1849 owned by a relative is presently on loan to the Dacorum Heritage Trust Ltd in Berkhamsted. This set is absent the four etchings of the Scotland scenes, but has *At Catdown near Plymouth* and *A Sketch on the North Western Railway,* two additional scenes not found in either of the sets at the British Museum. A close examination of this set shows the handwritten name L. J. Cranstone with the date 1849 present on six of the etchings; two have only the name L. J. Cranstone visible, two have the initials LJC present. No name, initials or dates can be discerned on the other four etchings.

A fourth set of fifteen of the 1849 and 1854 dated etchings donated by a direct descendant of Cranstone is owned by the John Oxley Library in Brisbane, Australia. It is most likely the set was brought to Australia when Cranstone immigrated there in 1883.

Additional Paintings

The 1851 British Census confirms that Cranstone was temporarily in Plymouth on March 31, 1851, the date the census was taken throughout the country, as it included him as a visitor at the residence of William Newberry, a white or tin smith. Cranstone's profession was given as portrait painter and he was most likely painting the Newberry family at the time. Cranstone prepared several of the seventeen etchings published in 1849 in Plymouth and may have come to the Newberry family's attention at that time.[75]

In 1854, Cranstone exhibited the oil, *Cheap Jack* at the Royal Academy.[76] His address was listed on the exhibit's catalog as 12, St. Mark's Street, Summershill, Birmingham. Cranstone returned to Hemel Hempstead sometime after this date and about 1855 painted the oil, *Hemel Hempstead Market Place.* The couple depicted to the right, are Cranstone's younger brother, Edmund, and Miss E. Donaldson, who wed on December 13, 1856. At the time, her parents were the owners of the Swan Inn on High Street.[77]

5.13 *Hemel Hempstead Market Place,* c. 1855, oil on fabric, 15 ½ x 12 ½ in. Courtesy, David Crantone and Dacorum Heritage Trust Ltd, Berkhamsted, England

Cranstone's Marriage

On July 4, 1855 Cranstone, now thirty-three, married Lillia Messenger, thirty-two, at Saint Mary's Church in Hemel Hempstead.[78] Cranstone probably met Lillia while she was teaching at the boarding school on Marlowes she operated with her older sister, Ann.[79] Born in nearby Welwyn, Hertfordshire, they were the daughters of Thomas and Annie Messenger. At the time of the wedding, the Messengers and their sons William and George manufactured rope and twine in the Boxmoor section of Hemel Hempstead.[80]

5.14 *Lillia Messenger Cranstone*, c. 1859, daguerreotype. Courtesy, Richmond Art Museum, Richmond, Indiana.

After their marriage, the Cranstones lived at Hill House on the Redbourn Road in Hemel Hempstead. Here, Lillia established a boarding school where Lefevre taught art and drawing. About 1866, the Cranstones moved to the "White House" at 51 Marlowes in Hemel Hempstead [81] where they lived and Lillia ran the boarding school until her death in 1882. The building, a large Georgian house with a three storied semicircular bay on each side of the entrance, had previously been a ladies' boarding school run by Georgiana Innes.[82] To do his part, Lefevre continued teaching art and drawing at the school.

5.15 *The "White House,"* Hemel Hempstead, England, 2002, photo, Courtesy, the author

    The last painting on record exhibited by Cranstone in England was *Reading the Scriptures* in 1867 at the Royal Society for British Artists in Suffolk Street. [83] His address was listed in the exhibition catalog as "Cornbrook House," Hemel Hempstead, but according to his nephew, [84] this is erroneous as by then Cranstone actually resided at the "White House" in Marlowes, Hemel Hempstead. Other oil paintings by Cranstone include the *Tythe Collector* (date unknown), oil on fabric, 31.0 x 41.0 in., sold as Lot 214 in 1973 by Biddle and Webb of Birmingham, England [85] and *Vacant Chair*, 1858, oil on fabric, 20.0 x 16.0 in. sold as lot 183 by James Lawson in Sydney, Australia in April 2001. [86]

6

Australia, 1883-1893

Not much is known about Cranstone's life after 1867 other than that he continued to teach at his wife's school. The year 1882, however, was one of emotion and change for Cranstone beginning with the death of Lillia, his wife of twenty-seven years, on July 12th at age fifty-nine. She is buried at Heath Lane Cemetery in Hemel Hempstead where her gravesite is marked by a simple stone marker beginning to show the effects of time.

6.1 *Lillia Cranstone Tombstone*, Heath Lane Cemetery, Hemel Hempstead, 2001, photo. Courtesy, the author

Lillia's death led to the closing of the private school she ran in the "White House" at 51 Marlowes, Hemel Hempstead that apparently was already in financial straits.[87] Cranstone and his children, seventeen-year-old daughter Beatrice Lillia and twenty-three year old son, Frederick George, no doubt discussed their future. Their decision to immigrate to Australia was likely influenced by the plans of his oldest son William, now a medical doctor, to move there. William had studied medicine in London and was elected to membership in the Royal College of Surgeons and Licensed Societies of Apothecaries in 1881.[88] In 1882, he secured the position of chief surgeon at the Peak Downs Hospital in the gold mining town of Clermont, about 460 miles northwest of Brisbane.

William, however, had one more duty to perform before departing and on 17 October 1882, he married Miss Ellen Kent.[89] Four days later they and the rest of the family sailed from London bound for Sydney on the three-masted clipper ship, the *Ann Duthie*.[90] The passenger list indicates that Dr. William Cranstone was employed as the ship's surgeon while the Cranstone family traveled as passengers in the saloon or first class. [91]

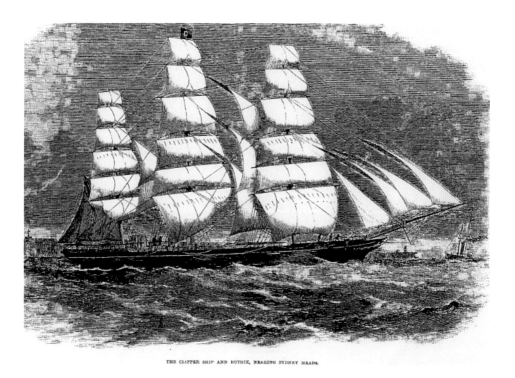

THE CLIPPER SHIP ANN DUTHIE, NEARING SYDNEY HEADS.

6.2 *The Clipper Ship Ann Duthie, Nearing Sydney Heads,* 1869, Illustrated Sydney News, Jan 21, 1869. Courtesy, Mitchell Library, State Library of New South Wales, Australia

Arrival in Sydney, Australia

The ninety-day voyage around the Cape of Good Hope brought them to the Heads outside Sydney harbor late on the evening of January 17, 1883. A tug took the *Ann Duthie* to Watson's Bay where she was forced to anchor for the night because the assistant health officer was not available. Early the next morning, the ship and passengers were officially cleared at Neutral Bay near Sydney. Captain George Morgan's report noted two incidents during the trip. On November 14, Major Phillips, a saloon passenger, jumped overboard at 11:30 p.m. He had been ill, consequently the captain conjectured Phillips took his own life. The *Ann Duthie* had a narrow escape on December 19, 1882 when thick clouds prevented proper bearings from being taken. As a result, the ship came within a half-mile of going aground on rocks near the Twelve Apostles region of the Crozet Islands in the southern Indian Ocean.[92] Frederick also kept a diary commenting, that it was a dull trip except for the excitement generated by Major Phillip's death and the night Captain Morgan found Beatrice in the saloon after walking in her sleep.[93]

Before departing on the next leg of their journey, the Cranstone family spent a day in the Sydney area. Curious about his new homeland, Lefevre toured the area to capture some of its scenery in his first pen-and-ink sketches of Australia. The Dacorum Heritage Trust Ltd, Berkhamsted, England collection houses five 12 ¾ x 8 in. sketches including two of Fairy Bower at the seashore town of Manly and one each of the suburb of Balmain, Sydney Harbor, and the Parramatta River.

6.3 *Fairy Bower, Manly, Sydney*, 1883, pen and ink drawing, 12 ¾ x 9 ¼ in. Courtesy, David Cranstone and Dacorum Heritage Trust Ltd, Berkhamsted, England

6.4 *Sydney Harbor*, 1883, pen and ink drawing, 12 ¾ x 8.0 in. Courtesy, David Cranstone and Dacorum Heritage Trust Ltd, Berkhamsted, England

6.5 *Parramatta River, Sydney*, 1883, pen and ink drawing, 12 ¾ x 9.0 in. Courtesy, David Crantone and Dacorum Heritage Trust Ltd, Berkhamsted, England

The Peak Downs Hospital, Clermont

From Sydney, the family took a coastal ship to the port of Rockhampton, Queensland, some 810 miles north. They completed their journey to Clermont on February 20, 1883, having traveled 221 miles overland by stagecoach from Rockhampton. The local paper reported their arrival and that the town's current physician, Dr. Ray, would be departing soon.[94]

Dr. William Cranstone received his registration by the Queensland Medical Board in early April 1883 as a duly qualified medical practitioner.[95] In addition to establishing a private practice, he began his new posting as chief surgeon at the Peak Downs Hospital. William also became quite involved in Clermont's social activities. He developed a keen interest in horse racing, owned several racehorses, and over the next few years was both the chairman and a committee member of the Peak Downs Turf Club, a committee member of the School of Arts, the first president of the chess club, and was elected vice-president of the Peak Downs Pastoral and Agricultural Society. In 1887, William founded and served as first chairman of the Clermont Club, a social club for the town's leading citizens.[96]

Dr. Cranstone became well known locally as an expert in the treatment of gold- bearing ores and in October 1885 became the first chairman of the Cement Hill Gold Mining Co., Ltd.[97] The company did not fare well in recovering gold from the Cement Hill, Spring Rush goldfield near Clermont and went into liquidation in 1887.

Art Exhibitions at the Rockhampton School of Arts

Lefevre's interest in art continued while he, Frederick, and Beatrice lived with William and his wife at the doctor's residence adjacent to the Peak Downs Hospital. While Clermont did not have any opportunities to display his art, one did develop in Rockhampton now reachable by train. In 1884, the Rockhampton School of Arts planned to expand their building. Faced with a monetary shortfall of several hundred pounds, the school decided to hold an exhibition of local products of art and manufacturing from August 26-30, 1884. Cranstone was not eligible for the competitive portion because the section was open only for artwork prepared in Australia. However, he did enter examples done in England in the section designated as art lent for exhibition only. From the description in the local newspaper these were most likely some of the sixty illustrations in a scrapbook now at the John Oxley Library in Brisbane. Each consists of a phrase from poems by Keats, Tennyson, Cowper, Wordsworth, Longfellow and others coupled with a pen and ink drawing. The Rockhampton newspaper reported that: "We must not omit to mention the etchings illustrative of select lines of poetry. These are from the pen of Mr. Cranstone, we understand, and are works of art of a very high character. The illustrations are singularly beautiful, and convey far more to the mind than the words attached to them." [98]

"———— embosomed soft in trees"

Thomson.

6.6 *Illustrated Poem by Thomson*, c. 1865, watercolor, 9.0 x 11 ¼ in. Courtesy, Collection: John Oxley Library, State Library of Queensland, Australia

Lefevre entered four new works of local scenes in the Paintings and Drawings section in the 2nd annual arts exhibition held August 25-29, 1885, taking home awards for three of the four entries. While his oil painting depicting a bush road near Clermont did not garner a prize, Cranstone did receive an award for his crayon drawing of Peak Downs Hospital and the nearby landscape. The local newspaper described this drawing as ". . .without doubt one of the best and most carefully finished pictures in competition." [99] He also won prizes for his pen-and-ink sketch of a landscape, *The Lagoon, Clermont,* and for an etching of a landscape from nature, *The Ferry Boat.*[100]

Lefevre's participation in the Rockhampton School of Arts exhibitions was his first in Australia and may have been the first since he exhibited *Reading The Scriptures* almost twenty years earlier. Unfortunately, the 1884 and 1885 exhibitions were probably his last because the school's poor financial situation prevented it from sponsoring other exhibitions before Cranstone's departure from Clermont in 1889.[101]

While living in Clermont, Lefevre also prepared a number of pen-and-ink drawings of local landscapes, including three sketches currently in the Dacorum Heritage Trust Ltd collection titled *Retro, Queensland; Fairview; Wolfang, Queensland;* and *Near Clermont.* In addition, a relative in New Zealand owns two pen-and-ink sketches, the *Hospital and Residence, Clermont,* and the *Hospital, Clermont.* [102]

6.7 *Retro, Queensland,* c. 1885, pen and ink drawing, 12 ¾ x 9.0 in. Courtesy, David Cranstone and Dacorum Heritage Trust Ltd, Berkhamsted, England

6.8 *Fairview, Wolfang, Queensland*, c.1885, pen and ink drawing, 12 ¾ x 9.0 in. Courtesy, David Cranstone and Dacorum Heritage Trust Ltd, Berkhamsted, England

6.9 *Near Clermont*, c.1885, pen and ink drawing, 12 ¾ x 9.0 in. Courtesy David Cranstone and Dacorum Heritage Trust Ltd, Berkhamsted, England

Lefevre also painted scenes near Emu Park, a small seashore town about fifteen miles northeast of Rockhampton. Lefevre's images of the Emu Park area include three watercolor paintings and an artist's sketchbook with forty-one pen and ink drawings at the Oxley Library; two pen-and-ink drawings sold in 1987 to an unknown party, [103] and sixteen watercolor scenes sold at Christie's Melbourne in 1972, also to an unknown buyer.[104]

Cranstone's Family in Australia

Existing editions of the *Peak Downs Telegram* published in Clermont indicate little happened in the lives of the Cranstone family between 1885 and early 1888. William continued as the hospital surgeon and kept up his social activities. By February 1888, however, William had developed an unknown medical condition that led him to request a nine-month leave of absence from the hospital. An article in the local newspaper announced his departure on a trip to Europe "for the benefit of his health" and hoped that "the popular doctor would also take the opportunity to update himself on the latest medical advances." [105] At a farewell dinner, Dr. Cranstone was described as ". . .a man who knows a lot and talks a lot, tireless, capital company, never absent and never the subject of complaint." [106] His friends wished him well on his return to London, a speedy recovery, and hoped to see him again in Clermont. During William's absence, it appears that Lefevre and his children continued to live at the hospital residence.

In November 1888, William was granted an additional three months absence. He returned to Clermont with his wife, small children, and nursemaid on April 16, 1889, and immediately resumed his duties as the hospital surgeon. [107] However, on December 3, 1889 William resigned his position and moved his family on December 16, 1889 to Melbourne, Victoria, where he established a practice. [108] William died September 18, 1906, of a cerebral abscess at age fifty in Melbourne Hospital. William and Ellen had a son, Thomas, who died at a young age and two daughters, Eleanor Lillia and Mary, who married and lived full lives in Australia. [109]

In 1888, William's brother, Frederick, moved to northern Queensland. Frederick's daughter Nancy Rose Cranstone wrote that he "…was going to settle on the land and went to North Queensland right up in the part that was wild then, Blacks all around." [110] In 1889, he was listed as a sugar planter at Mossman River at a point eight miles by boat north of Port Douglas, Queensland. [111]

Frederick's death certificate indicates he relocated to Melbourne from North Queensland in 1891. In her letter, Nancy, mentions her father changed his mind about settling in the north and moved to Melbourne where he found employment with the Commercial Bank of Australia. Frederick was sent as branch manager to Berwick, Victoria, where he met his future wife, Winifred Nellie Symonds, who he married in 1898. They had two children, Edward Lefevre Cranstone, who became a well known World War II cinematographer, and Nancy Rose, who in 1948 owned a cake shop in the Toorak section of Melbourne. Frederick died of prostatitis at age sixty on July 28, 1919, [112] in Melbourne Hospital while Edward Lefevre Cranstone died at eighty-five at his home in Artarmon near Sydney on November 22, 1988. [113] In 1993 at age 84, Nancy Cranstone lived in Mornington, Victoria.

Lefevre and Beatrice Cranstone Move to Brisbane

Lefevre and his daughter, Beatrice (known as Aunt Trissie to her family), moved to Brisbane in 1889 at the time William moved to Melbourne. As the lone daughter, the role of caretaker for her aging father fell to Beatrice who became a dressmaker in Wakefield's Building on Adelaide Street in Brisbane. [114] She and Lefevre lived at Clydebank Cottage on North Quay, most likely renting rooms from the owner, Mrs. S. Learmouth. [115] After her father's death, Beatrice moved to the town of Mackay north of Brisbane.

On May 25, 1897, at age thirty-one, she married Graham Augustus Turnor, a forty-three year old widower.[116] He was a "grazier" or cattle rancher and they lived on a cattle station called Bolingbroke near Mackay. They had two children, Edmund and Edmunda Lillia, who attended school near Melbourne while staying at Uncle Frederick's home, subsequently returning to Queensland where they spent their adult years. Graham Turnor, who died about 1938, was described by his niece, Nancy Cranstone as ". . .wild in his youth and seemed a bit eccentric but was a darling, well read English gentleman." Beatrice was known to be living in Brisbane in 1948.

Lefevre did a large number of pen-and-ink sketches of Brisbane City, South Brisbane, and the suburb of Toowang that are in three artists sketchbooks in the John Oxley Library. Each book appears to cover a year's worth of sketching. The first book contains thirty-two sketches, the second twenty-one sketches, and the third thirty-two, for a total of eighty-five sketches of Brisbane. These three sketchbooks and a fourth containing the forty-one Emu Park drawings were donated to the John Oxley Library, Brisbane, in 1968 by Miss E. Turnor of that city most likely Edmunda Lillia Turnor, the artist's granddaughter.

6.10 *Brisbane – Leichhardt St,* c. 1890, pen and ink drawing, 5 7/8 x 8 5/8 in. Courtesy, Collection: John Oxley Library, State Library of Queensland, Australia

6.11 *Brisbane,* c. 1890, pen and ink drawing, 5 7/8 x 8 5/8 in. Courtesy, Collection: John Oxley Library, State Library of Queensland, Australia

6.12 *Milton – Brisbane*, c. 1890, 5 7/8 x 8 5/8 in. Courtesy, Collection: John Oxley Library, State Library of Queensland, Australia

Death of Lefevre James Cranstone in Brisbane

Cranstone's health declined in his final years and he was almost blind at the time of his death. Lefevre James Cranstone died at 2 p.m. June 22, 1893 at the age of seventy-one at his residence, Clydebank Cottage, North Quay, Brisbane.[117] His death certificate lists the cause as senile decay and increasing debility.[118] Burial took place the same day with Beatrice in attendance at the Toowang Cemetery (now the Brisbane General Cemetery). Cranstone is buried in Portion 2A, Section 15, Plot 22. The spelling of his given name on the tombstone is incorrect; it should be Lefevre rather than Le Fevre. This latter spelling can also be found on the official death certificate, most likely the source for the name on the tombstone.

6.13 Tombstone of Lefevre James Cranstone, Brisbane General Cemetery, Brisbane, Australia, 2002, photo, Courtesy, the author

EPILOGUE

My journey to Brisbane in January 2002 allowed me to pay respects to this wonderful artist whose life and art I have come to know. I had earlier journeyed to Hemel Hempstead in November 2001 to visit the grave of his wife, Lillia. Through touching the tombstones that guard each of their graves, I was able to bridge the distance that had separated this husband and wife for well over a century. Telling their story has equally been a very satisfying journey and one I hope you have enjoyed.

Letter to Hemel Hemstead Gazette
dated December 29, 1860

Gentlemen, - Will you allow one who has recently returned from America to offer a few remarks on the state of that country, particularly in reference to Slavery?

The election of Mr. Lincoln as President of the United States is an event of great importance. Hitherto the Southern States by the threat of disunion have coerced the North into electing a pro-slavery President; but this time the threat has failed, and the States of Georgia and Carolina are talking loudly of seceding from the federation, but it is to be hoped that they will be wise in time and submit to the decision of the majority, without which compliance no representative government can exist.

The present state of political parties in America hangs simply on the slavery questions, and it must be a matter of rejoicing to all the friends of progress to find a party which the last few years have rendered powerful in organization and strong in numerical force, and which is backed by the greatest intellects in America, stemming the tide of slavery, and seeking to keep within its present limits the encroachments of the Democrats. The party I allude to, the Republican, nicknamed Black Republican by their opponents, have within the last few years obtained that position that has enabled them to place an anti-slavery President at the head of the Republic. Thus we have Republicans on the one hand striving to stem the tide of slavery, and the Democrats seek still further to extend it. To possess a Cuba, --to make filibustering expeditions against neighboring states, to coerce all the newly acquired territories, and by all and every means to spread slavery, are the principal points in the creed of the latter party, a party that has now governed the country for a number of years. The Democracy, hitherto so powerful, unscrupulous, and corrupt have at length failed to elect their candidate. The John Brown raid has had the effect under the influence of a reign of terror of tightening the chains of the slave, and has led to a more rigid surveillance of all suspected of abolitionism. All republican papers, even of the mildest flavor, subscribed for by men in the South, are stopped at the post-office. All post-masters have the power of seizing newspapers they choose to think contain incendiary matter, and these irresponsible individuals are not slow in availing themselves of the power which the law has placed in their hands. The *New York Tribune*, edited by Horace Greely, is particularly obnoxious in the South, and one seen with this paper would subject himself to the tender mercies of Judge Lynch. The boasted unanimity of the South, in opposition to Black Republicanism, is similar to that which exists in France and Austria, and which is maintained by like means. There are but very few avowed Republicans in the Slave States, simply because no one can be an active Republican and stay in them, except along the borders, unless he takes his life in his hand and holds it at the mouth of the pistol. Thousands who would subscribe for anti-slavery papers are deterred from doing so by terror. The anti-slavery party is daily defamed in fifteen states of the Union, but are not allowed a hearing in reply. The circulation of the facts whereon they rest the justification of their faith entails prosecution and punishment as for the crime of felony. To advocate their principles at all would subject the printing press to the tender mercies of mob law. The expression of any opinion bearing on this subject would expose free white men to be hunted like wild beasts. John Van Buren is said to have remarked lately that there is no despotism in Europe which could compare in cruelty and meanness with that now tyrannizing in the slave states, and gave as a reason that the European despots had such a number of subjects that they were obliged to establish some general rules of action, while an enlightened public sentiment, together with the desire of maintaining a character for generosity, had given to their conduct some show of justice and liberality. But your little one-horse despots are not restrained by any such considerations, and do not govern by anything so respectable as their absolute will—being often controlled more by the merest caprice. Many occurrences furnish evidence in confirmation of these views. John B. Brown is a farmer and dairyman residing near Washington, and has supplied a goodly portion of the citizens of Washington with milk and other necessary products of his well-cultivated land. One day last June he procured from the Post Office his papers, the "New York Tribune," the "Baltimore Sun," and "Washington Star". Such is the lynx-espionage of the paramount despotism, that Mr. Brown, on his way home, was seized, searched, and for having these terrible publications in his pockets, he was hurried down to the city of Alexandria, and compelled to give bail in two-thousand dollars to escape confinement in the common jail. But many persons do not get off so easily. James Power, a working stone mason employed in the Capitol at Charleston, South Carolina, once remarked to a fellow-workman that a poor white man was not considered any better than a nigger. For this observation he was sent to the city gaol for six days, brought out and whipped half naked in the streets by a colored man, tarred and feathered, and finally put into a railway car, and sent to New York; but several times on the road a ferocious and brutal mob tarred and feathered him afresh, and he arrived finally in New York and was there when I left the country in one of the hospitals of that place. These facts are taken from several southern papers, given forth with such zest as if they thought it a capital joke. Space will not allow me to go further into details; now and then such startling things appear in the papers, making every humane man recoil with horror—tales of tarring, feathering, hanging, and burning, by Judge Lynch. We venture to say that neither Austria nor Naples, in the palmist days of their tyranny, ever exceeded these outrages upon personal freedom. And what must be the character of a social system, that shows such horror on the part of the people to read Anti-slavery publications? May we not say of such despots, in the language of an ancient volume, 'Ye hate the light because your deeds are evil.' Take another case just developed in Kentucky, where a son-in-law and two or three grandchildren of an aged slaveholder named Southerland have joined in a suit to compel him to continue as a slaveholder against his own conscience and will, and his relations have instituted legal proceedings to prevent him from manumitting his own slaves. The case came on for trial at the Casey Circuit Court, but was adjourned. Where are the RIGHTS OF PROPERTY, when a free white citizen is thus treated? If it is so important to secure a landholder's right to his own negroes in Nebraska, why should not he be afforded a kindred liberty to "do as he likes with his own" in Kentucky also.

A few words as to State legislation. Take for example the state of Virginia, and the same might be applied to other slave states also, who have suffered more or less under the steady yearly encroachment of slave capital upon the personal rights of the laboring white man. The non-slaveholding farmers and mechanics, and working men of Virginia are oppressed and weighted down with taxation for the benefit of slave capitalists, merely because the latter have the political power, and choose to exercise its tyranny without mercy. Capital in the shape of slaves under Virginia Democratic legislation, is made to pay but about 300,000 dollars towards the expenses of the state, whereas, if it was taxed as other capital is, it would be made to contribute at least 1,200,000 dollars. The products of the slave labour of Virginia consisting altogether of tobacco, corn, wheat, and oats are exempt, too, from taxation, whilst the products of the white labour of the non-slaveholding part of the state, consisting of cattle, sheep, hogs &e, are made to contribute largely to the state treasury. Whilst also, the slave under 12 years of age is held by these mis-called rulers, of Virginia as privileged property, and as such is free from all taxation, though he may be worth a thousand or more dollars, the young colts, calves, lambs and pigs, of the Virginian farmers are regularly listed by the commissions of the revenue, and made to contribute to the public treasury. And whilst the owner of a slave over 12 years of age, and worth on a fair average 1200 dollars, is taxed for him the small pittance of 1 dollar 20 cents, the small merchant even with a capital as meager as 600 dollars, is made to pay the first year the onerous tax of 60 dollars, and after that an enormous percentage on his sales. And even the white labouring man, though he may own no capital at all, be he a mechanic, day laborer or only a casual hand in a harvest field, is made to contribute a percentage on his hard earned wages in order that the privileged property of Virginian taskmasters may not be compelled to pay its just share to the public expense; and wherever we turn our eyes we see this unequal and unjust exemption, following the line of slave property. Why, if a bull or a steer of a Virginian farmer becomes vicious, so as to be a public nuisance, it is ordered by the law to be killed, and the loss falls upon the owner and on him alone; but if it happens that a slave becomes vicious, and commits crime, he is hanged or transported, and it is provided by the law that his owner shall be paid his assessed value out of the state treasury. Many other aggressions of the black capitalists upon the property and labour of the non-slave-holding white men, (committed under the banner of Democracy), could be pointed out, but this is sufficient to show how ten thousand persons, *simply by reason of their slave capital,* have as great a representation as forty thousand of other freeman, and how they can wield the power of the state, and load the white industry of the country with burdens grievous to be borne. If the course of Virginia legislation is arbitrary to the white man, it must be conceded that slavery in that state is in a mild form. Ill-treatment of the slaves is an exception, not the rule. The master that abuses the power thus placed in his hands is amenable to the law of public opinion, and the public are not slow to stigmatize any wanton abuse of power. Unlike free negroes the slave is well fed, not hard worked, and in most cases indulgently treated. But it is in the slave auction rooms where the horrors of the system are most palpable to the eye. No pen can adequately describe scenes so revolting to the mind of a stranger. It was in the month of March of this present year, that being at Richmond, Virginia, I turned down a back street and saw a row of dirty looking houses to the doors of which were posted red flags on which were pinned pieces of paper announcing the time of sale of the human merchandise within. Entering one of these low dens in company with a motley crowd, the first object that met the eye was a company of coloured women and young girls, seated on benches awaiting the sale. The men and boys are placed behind a screen at the further end of the room, surrounded by an eager crowd of purchasers, each slave being stripped to the waist, that he may be tested as to soundness and bodily health. The sale room was long, dark and dingy, with a raised platform on one side for the salesman and the "lot." Awaiting the arrival for the auctioneer these goods are freely handled and inspected. Here is every shade of complexion from purest ebony to white, black field hands, yellow beauties, stout fellows; if the buyer wishes bright-eyed, smooth of skin, supple of form, full-chested, clean-limbed creatures, culinary prodigies, deft semptresses (sic), delightful washerwomen, charioteers, unrivalled, the very treasures of commercial christianity; the only adequate exponents of Virginian wealth and enterprise. The women are dressed in flaunting gay colours, the men in their best trim. The auctioneer arrives, the sale commences. I see one after another mount the platform— the men first, the women and children last. And they are quickly knocked down, showing a brisk demand in the market. Whilst the sale is progressing each slave is subjected to a close examination; their arms and hands are felt— teeth inspected—made to walk up and down the room, and to mount and remount the platform. In spite of what is so often said in contradiction to the parting of families, I was an eyewitness that such is the fact; several young children and their mothers being knocked down to different purchasers. With a long-drawn breath I follow the crowd out, who made their way to another room, where the same scene is enacted. Day after day these scenes are going on in the midst of churches and chapels, and within a stone's throw of a splendid monument of Washington.

In traveling through the slave states one cannot help being struck with the general air of decadence and ruin in comparison with the Northern states—so prosperous in wealth and population. The blighting consequences of slavery are everywhere visible, cursing the land with its baneful effects. Public morals, and the general property of the South—which it is the province of the government to a great extent to protect and cherish—are deplorably injured by slavery, from the fact that the possession and management of slaves from a source of endless vexation and misery within the house, and waste and ruin on the farm, and that the youth of many parts of the south are growing up with a contempt of steady industry as a low service thing, which contempt induces idleness and all its attendant effeminacy, vice and worthlessness. The Southern states have already lapsed at each decade behind some of their free state rivals not possessing their natural capabilities; and unless some provision is made for the gradual riddance of this consuming evil, the American Union will never obtain its true position amongst the leading nations of the world.

> I am, Gentlemen,
> Your obedient servant,
> L.J.C.

EXHIBITIONS OF CRANSTONE'S PAINTINGS IN AMERICA, ENGLAND AND AUSTRALIA

UNITED STATES:

1. Hirsch and Adler Galleries, Inc. 21 East 67 St., New York, N.Y. "The American Scene: A Survey of the Life and Landscape of the 19th Century," October 29 through November 22, 1969. James Lefevre Cranstone. Exhibit item 14a. *Winter Scene near Richmond, Indiana,* watercolor 6.0 x 12.0 in. (sight). Exhibit item 14b. *Paddlesteamers on the Ohio River,* watercolor 7.0 x 11 ½ in. (sight).

2. Indianapolis Museum of Art, Indianapolis, Indiana. "Mirages of Memory: 200 Years of Indiana Art." Indianapolis Museum of Art, November 6, 1976 – January 2, 1977. Items six and seven are both titled *Street Scene in Richmond, Indiana,* watercolor and pencil, 6 ½ x 11.0 in. Items lent by the Indiana Historical Society Library.

3. Art Gallery, University of Notre Dame, South Bend, Indiana. January 16-March 20, 1977. Same art exhibit, "Mirages of Memory: 200 Years of Indiana Art," described above held at the Indianapolis Museum of Art, November 6, 1976 – January 2, 1977.

4. Oglebay Institute Mansion Museum, Wheeling, West Virginia. "Lefevre J. Cranstone's Views of Antebellum America." Exhibition of Cranstone watercolors at the Oglebay Institute Mansion Museum, June 16, 1984 – August 12, 1984.

5. Parkersburg Art Center, Parkersburg, West Virginia. September 7 – October 13, 1985. Same Cranstone exhibit described above, "Lefevre J. Cranstone's Views of Antebellum America," held at the Oglebay Institute Mansion Museum from June 16, 1984 – August 12, 1984.

6. Memorial Art Gallery of the University of Rochester, Rochester, New York, June 16-August 12, 1984. "The Course of Empire – The Erie Canal and the New York Landscape." Contains two watercolors by Lefevre James Cranstone on loan from the Museum of Fine Arts, Boston, M. and M. Karolik Collection. Item ten is *Frontier Mills, Buffalo, New York (I),* watercolor on paper, 6 3/8 x 11 1/8 in. and item eleven is *Frontier Mills, Buffalo, New York (II),* 6 ½" X 11 1/8".

7. The Museum of the Confederacy, Richmond, Virginia, July-December 1991. Exhibit "Before Freedom Came: African American Life in the Antebellum South, 1795-1865," included Lefevre James Cranstone's *Slave Auction Virginia* on loan from the Virginia Historical Society.

8. Virginia Historical Society, Richmond, Virginia, Oct. 6, 1993 – May 31, 1994. Exhibit "Away I'm Bound Away – Virginia and the Westward Movement" included Lefevre James Cranstone's *Slave Auction, Virginia*.

9. Richmond Art Museum, Richmond, Indiana. "LeFevre Cranstone: An Outsider's View of the Simple Beauty of Richmond, Indiana." Sept. 26 - Nov. 5, 1998. Exhibit of L. J. Cranstone watercolors sponsored by Indiana University (IU) East and IU Lilly Library, Bloomington.

10. Virginia Historical Society, Richmond, Virginia. "The Virginia Landscape: A Cultural History," Exhibit at the Virginia Historical Society, July 13, 2000 – November 12, 2000.

11. Virginia Historical Society, Richmond, Virginia. "Treasures Revealed from the Paul Mellon Library of America," Exhibit at the Virginia Historical Society, September 21, 2001 - January 20, 2002.

12. Virginia Historical Society, Richmond, Virginia. "Old Virginia: The Pursuit of a Pastoral Ideal," Exhibit at the Virginia Historical Society, February 8, 2003 - June 8, 2003.

ENGLAND:
1. "The Exhibition of the Royal Academy," London, England, 1845. Item 660, *Country Fair* oil painting by Lefevre James Cranstone.

2. "Exhibition at the Royal Society of British Artists in Suffolk Street," London, U.K., 1847. Item 414, oil painting *The Lace Maker*, L. J. Cranstone.

3. "The Exhibition of the Royal Academy," London, England, 1850. Item 424, *Waiting at the Station* oil painting by Lefevre James Cranstone.

4. "The Exhibition of the Royal Academy," London, U.K., 1854. Item 1236, *Cheap Jack*, oil painting by Lefevre James Cranstone.

5. "Exhibition at the British Institution," London, U.K., 1856. Item 15, *News of the War,* oil painting by L. J. Cranstone.

6. "Exhibition at the Royal Society of British Artists in Suffolk Street," London, U.K., 1863. Item 254, *Slave Auction, Virginia*, oil painting by L.J. Cranstone.

7. "Exhibition at the Royal Society of British Artists in Suffolk Street," London, U.K., 1867. Item 204, *Reading the Scriptures*, oil painting by L. J. Cranstone.

8. M. Newman Ltd., London, U.K. circa 1965. Advertisements in Connoisseur, March 1965 and Apollo, August 1965. Oil painting signed and dated 1850 *Waiting at the Station* by Lefevre J. Cranstone. Canvas size: 26.0 x 42.0 in.

9. Leger Galleries, 13 Old Bond Street, London, UK, 7 February – 16 March 1968. "Truth to Nature Exhibition," oil painting on canvas 24.0 x 36.0 in. by L. J. Cranstone titled: *Harpers Ferry: A View of the Town on the Potomac River, West Virginia.*

10. Oscar and Peter Johnson Limited, Lowndres Lodge Gallery, 27 Lowndres Street, London, SW 1, UK, exhibited at the Antique Dealers's Fair, Grosvenor House, June 12-17, 1968, oil painting on canvas, 24.0 x 36.0 in. by L. J. Cranstone titled: *Harpers Ferry on the Potomac River, West Virginia.*

AUSTRALIA:

1. "First Annual Exhibition of the Rockhampton School of Arts," Rockhampton, Queensland, Australia held 26-30 August 1884. Lefevre James Cranstone exhibited several drawings brought from England including a drawing illustrating poetry.

2. "Second Annual Exhibition of the Rockhampton School of Arts", Rockhampton, Queensland, Australia held 25-29 August 1885. Lefevre James Cranstone entered four new works of art of scenes prepared near the town of Clermont, Australia. They are:
a. Oil painting of a bush road near Clermont.
b. A crayon drawing titled *The Peak Downs Hospital, Clermont.*
c. Pen and ink sketch titled *The Lagoon, Clermont.*
d. An etching titled *The Ferry Boat.*

AUCTIONS OF CRANSTONE'S PAINTINGS IN AMERICA, ENGLAND AND AUSTRALIA

UNITED STATES:

1. Sotheby's Chicago, 215 W. Ohio St., Chicago, IL. Sale dated October 19-21, 1997. Furniture, Decorations, Jewelry and Paintings, Watercolor by Lefevre James Cranstone titled *Ohio River, Wheeling, Virginia*, 6 ½ x 12 ½ in., Lot 1112. Bought in.

2. Samuel T. Freeman & Co., 1808 Chestnut St., Philadelphia, Pa. Sale dated June 4, 2000. Property from Estate of Elizabeth Tukey, watercolor by Lefevre James Cranstone titled *Nr Wheeling*, 6 ½ x 11 ½ in., Lot 44.

ENGLAND:

1. Christie, Manson and Woods, 8 King St., St. James Square, London, England. Sale dated February 17, 1928. "Catalogue of Modern Pictures & Drawings, the Property of L.W. Williamson, Esq. also Modern Pictures & Water Colour Drawings from Various Sources." Lot 100 consigned by Mrs. D. A. Ball, Emsworth, Humberstone, Leicestershire, England consisted of Lefevre J. Cranstone's oil painting *Slave Market, Virginia 1862*. A Mr. Mason purchased the painting for ten pounds, ten shillings. See paragraph five below for subsequent sales of this painting.

2. Sotheby & Co., 34-35 New Bond Street, London, England. Sale dated March 29, 1933. "Catalogue of Valuable Engravings of the French School, An Interesting Series of American Views in Water-Colours by L. J. Cranstone, The Property of T. R. Robinson, Esq., 25, Campden Hill Gardens, W.8, London and Other Properties."
   a. Lots 39-76 consisting of 96 paintings. Size ranges in size from 6 ½ x 9 ¾ to 7.0 x 13.0 in.
   b. Lot 77. A series of etchings, 1849, title and thirteen plates, original portfolio.

3. Sotheby & Co., 34-35 New Bond Street, London, U. K. Sale dated November 20, 1963. Fine English Eighteenth and Nineteenth Century Drawings and Paintings, Other Properties: Lot 87, *Waiting At The Station,* oil, 25 ½ x 41 ¼ in., signed and indistinctively dated 1850, exhibit #424 at Royal Academy in 1850. Purchased by Patch for $1,120.00. Same painting offered for sale by M. Newman Ltd, London from March to August 1965. Present whereabouts unknown.

4. Sotheby & Co., 34-35 New Bond Street, London, U.K. Sale dated December 18, 1963. Old Master paintings and Eighteenth and Nineteenth Century drawings and Paintings, Other Properties including framed paintings of North American School by Lefevre James Cranstone:

   a. Lot 213. *Niagara River*, Canada shore, two steamers crossing, 6 ½ x15 ¾ in. Purchased by Colnaghi for $672.00.

   b. Lot 214. *James River, Richmond, Virginia*, paddle steamers and other craft near the banks. 6 ¾ x 13 in. Purchased by Colnaghi for $952.00.

   c. Lot 215. *Ohio River*, large steamers by moonlight, 7 1//8 x 11 ½ in.; 8.0 x 11 ½ in. (2). The pair purchased by Hahn for $952.00.

   d. Lot 216. *York River, Virginia, Biglers Mills*, a pair. Each approximately 6 ¼ x 12 ¾ in. (2). The pair purchased by Colnaghi for $1,176.00.

   e. Lot 217. *Richmond, Indiana*, two winter scenes, a pair. Each approximately 6 ¼ x 12 ¼ in. (2). The pair purchased by Hahn for $504.00.

5. Biddle & Webb, Birmingham, UK. August 3, 1973, Lot 214: Oil Painting *The Tythe Collector*, size 31.0 x 41.0 in. Sale price $882.00.

6. Sotheby & Co., 34-35 New Bond St., London, U.K. Sale dated October 24, 1990. Paintings, Watercolours and Drawings from America and other countries.   Lot 9, American School, mid 19th Century, *Slave Auction, Virginia 1862*; Oil on canvas 11 ¾ x 19 ½ in. with original frame. Inscribed and signed on stretcher: "Slave Auction" Virginia/Painted by I. Cranstone, Hemel Hempstead Hart." In July 1991 this painting was acquired by the Virginia Historical Society from Robert M. Hicklin, Jr., Inc., Charleston, South Carolina and is the same painting sold by Christie, Manson and Woods described in paragraph one above.

7. Sotheby & Co., 34-35 New Bond St., London, U.K. Sale dated September 15, 2000. The Property of The Hon. Clive and Anne Gibson Removed from Monmouth House, Hyde Park Gate, Lot 205, Lefevre James Crantone, A Group of Watercolours of Views on the Kent Coast including *Ladies by a Beach-Hut, Dumpton Gap Near Broadstairs, On the Beach at Margate* and *Figures on the Beach at Broadstairs,* watercolour over pencil (4), each approximately 4 ¾ x 7.0 in.

8. Anderson & Garland, Marlborough House, Marlborough

Crescent, Newcastle upon Tyne, U.K., Sale dated December 11, 2001. Lot 15, Hemel Hempstead and other topographical etchings by L. J. Cranstone 1849 (10).

AUSTRALIA:

1. Christie, Manson & Woods (Australia), 81 Collins Street, Melbourne, Victoria, Australia. Australian Historical and Contemporary Drawings and Paintings and Some European Paintings and Sculpture. Sale March 14-15, 1972 at "The Age" Gallery, 250 Spencer Street, Melbourne:

a. Lot 189, Lefevre James Cranstone, 19th century, *Keppel Island, Emu Park*. A panel of eight watercolours of Queensland landscapes from a sketchbook. Each is inscribed with place-name. Each 6 5/8 x 9 ½ in. Provenance: The artist's heirs. The artist was a British painter, engraver and illustrator who settled in Queensland, circa 1880.

b. Lot 190: *Keppel Island, Emu Park; Yeppoon; Fitzroy River, Rockhampton*. A panel of eight watercolors of Queensland landscapes from a sketchbook. Each is inscribed with place-name. Each 6 5/8 x 9 ½ in.

2. Deutscher Fine Art, 68 Drummond Street, Carlton, Victoria, Australia. Australian and Australia Related Art: 1830s-1970s, Wednesday 25 November – Friday 11 December 1987:

Lot 30: L. J. Cranstone. *The Lagoon, Emu park*, circa 1888, ink on paper, 8 ¾ x 12 ¾ in. Image inscribed: *Lagoon, Emu Park, Qd.*

Lot 31: L. J. Cranstone. *Emu Park, north of Rockhampton* C 1888, ink on paper. 8 ¾ x 12 ¾ in. Inscribed below image lower let: *Emu Park, Qd.*

3. James Lawson Gallery, Sydney, NSW, Australia. Exhibit: "3,000 A.D." dated April 23, 2001. Lot 183. Lefevre James Cranstone, Oil Painting *Vacant Chair* signed and dated 1858, size 20.0 x 16.0 in.

NOTES

Chapter 1

[1] E. Blunt & G.W. Blunt, *American Lloyds, Registry of American and Foreign Shipping.* (New York: E. & G. W. Blunt, 1862), p. 576. The 257 foot, 1515 ton, three masted bark Kangaroo was built in 1854 in Greenock, Scotland and was equipped with an oscillating steam engine.

[2] Passenger List for Ship *Kangaroo,* Sept. 20, 1859, National Archives and Records Administration, Microfilm M-237, Roll 195, College Park, Maryland.

[3] Arthur Cranstone, Family History Notes, D/Ece/F1, Hertfordshire Archives and Local Studies, Hertford, England.

[4] John A. Cuthbert. *Early Art and Artists in West Virginia: An Introduction and Biographical Dictionary* (Morgantown, West Virginia, West Virginia University Press, 2000).

[5] Ronald Vern Jackson, ed. *Virginia 1860 Federal Census*: (Accelerated Indexing Systems International, Salt Lake City, Utah: 1988), Vol. 1: *A thru K.*

[6] *Palladium-Item and Sun-Telegram*, (Richmond, Indiana.), Dec. 3, 1962.

[7] *Ibid*, Apr. 11, 1951.

[8] *Ibid.*

[9] The Art Weekly, published by "The Art Weekly" Publishing Co., London, pps. 6, 8, Sept. 13, 1928.

[10] Williamsburg, Virginia, Colonial Williamsburg Foundation Archives, Furnishings-Portraits & Prints 1928, B.F. Stevens & Brown, Ltd., London to John D. Rockefeller, Jr., Oct. 5, 1928.

[11] Williamsburg, Virginia, Colonial Williamsburg Foundation Archives, Furnishings-Portraits & Prints 1928, B.F. Stevens & Brown, Ltd., London to Prof. J .A. C. Chandler, Oct. 5, 1928.

[12] Williamsburg, Virginia, Colonial Williamsburg Foundation Archives, Furnishings-Portraits & Prints 1928, W. A. R. Goodwin, Williamsburg, Virginia. to Colonel Woods, Nov. 6, 1928.

[13] B. F. Stevens & Brown Sales Catalogue, London, 1942.

Chapter 2

[14] Lefevre James Cranstone, Collection of 296 Sketches, Lilly Library, Indiana University, Bloomington, Indiana.

[15] Cranstone, Family History Notes.

[16] 1861 British Census, National Archives, England, RG9/838/37/20.

[17] J. H. Newton, *History of The Pan-Handle: Historical Collections of the Counties of Ohio, Brooke, Marshall and Hancock, West Virginia*, (Wheeling, West Virginia. J. A. Caldwell, 1879).

[18] *Palladium-Item and Sun-Telegram*, (Richmond, Indiana.), Apr. 10, 1951.

[19] Richmond City Directory, Richmond, Indiana.,1860.

[20] *Richmond Jeffersonian*, (Indiana.), Dec. 4, 1862.

[21] *Richmond Palladium*, Dec. 3, 1928; *Richmond Item*, Dec. 4, 1928.

[22] Palladium-Item and Sun-Telegram, Apr. 18, 22, July 9, 10, 1947.

[23] Ibid., Apr. 9, 10, 11, 12, 13, 16, 17, 18, 19, 20, 1951.

[24] Ibid., Dec. 27, 1994.

[25] William Kloss, *Art in the White House: A Nation's Pride.* (Washington, D.C., White House Historical Association, 1992).

[26] Picture booklet of Richmond scenes, (Brooklyn, New York.: Albertype Co., 1906).

[27] Langhorne Gibson, *Cabell's Canal: The Story of the James River and Kanawha Canal*, (Richmond, Virginia: Commodore Press, 2000).

[28] John H. Salmon, ed., *The Guide to Historic Virginia*, (Richmond, Virginia: Page One, Inc., 2002).

[29] William Wade Hinshaw, *Encyclopedia of American Quaker Genealogy*, (Ann Arbor, Michigan, Friends Book and Supply House, 1950).

[30] Deed. Apr. 11, 1874, Deed Book 3, pp. 1-3, James City County Courthouse, Williamsburg, Virginia.

[31] John E. Selby, *Revolution in Virginia: 1775-1783* (Williamsburg, Virginia: The Colonial Williamsburg Foundation, 1988).

[32] A Brief Guide to Bruton Parish Church, Williamsburg, Virginia, 2001.

[33] *Wheeling Intelligencer*, Oct. 17, 1859.

[34] The Evergreens Cemetery web site, "About Us," www.theevergreenscemetery.com, 2002.

[35] Blunt and Blunt, *American Lloyds,* 1862. The Vigo, a rigged bark built in 1855, weighed 1,103 tons and had a 360 horsepower steam engine. The ship with a crew of 82 belonged to the Inman Line out of Liverpool.

[36] Castle Island brochure, (Washington, D.C., National Park Service, U. S. Department of the Interior, 2002).

Chapter 3

[37] *Hemel Hempstead Gazette*, Dec. 29, 1860, D/Ece/F108, Hertfordshire Archives and Local Studies, Hertford, England.

[38] Oil on canvas, 13 by 21 inches first exhibited as Item 254 at the Exhibition at the Royal Society of British Artists in Suffolk Street, UK, in 1863.

[39] Jane Johnson. *Works Exhibited at the Royal Society of British Artists 1824-1893,* (Woodbridge, Suffolk, Eng: Antique Collectors' Club, 1990).

[40] Christie, Manson and Woods Sale, Lot 100, Feb. 17, 1928.

[41] David Hackett Fischer and James C. Kelley. *Away I'm Bound Away*, (Richmond, Virginia., Virginia Historical Society, 1993).

[42] Estill Curtis Pennington. *Look Away, Reality and Sentiment in Southern Art*, (Peachtree Publishers, Ltd., Atlanta, Georgia, 1989).

[43] *Truth to Nature*, Leger Galleries, item No. l5, London, Feb. 7–Mar. 16, 1968; Loundes Lodge Gallery, Antique Dealers' Fair, London, June 12-27, 1968.

Chapter 4

[44] Sotheby's London Sale, lots 39-77, Mar. 29, 1933.

[45] Mandy Money, *Antiques in and About London, New York Sun*, Apr. 29, 1933.

[46] Williamsburg, Virginia, Colonial Williamsburg Foundation Archives, Furnishings-Portraits & Prints 1933, I. B. Lee to Kathryn I. Bowen, Apr. 26, 1933.

[47] Williamsburg, Virginia, Colonial Williamsburg Foundation Archives, Furnishings-Portraits & Prints 1933, Kenneth Chorley to Susan H. Nash, July 17, 1933.

[48] Stevens and Brown, London, bill of sale to Alexander W. Weddell, April 3, 1933, Virginia Historical Society, Richmond, Virginia.

[49] Virginia Museum of Fine Arts to Smith, Aug. 29, 2001.

[50] Indiana Historical Society to Smith, Aug. 18, 2001.

[51] Marjorie Hunter, *Mrs. Kennedy Leads Hunt for Art to Grace White House, New York Times,* Nov. 26, 1961.

[52] Senator and Mrs. John D. Rockefeller IV Collection to Smith, Mar. 28, 2002.

[53] *M. & M. Karolik Collection of American Water Colors & Drawings 1800-1875, Vol. II.* (Boston: Museum of Fine Arts, 1962).

[54] Oglebay Institute Mansion Museum, "Lefevre J. Cranstone's Views of Antebellum America," June 16-Aug.12, 1984.

[55] Brochure, Richmond Art Museum, Richmond, Indiana., 2001

[56] Sterling and Francine Clark Art Institute, Williamstown, Massachusetts to Smith, Apr. 30, 2002.

[57] Killam Memorial Library, Dalhousie University, Halifax, Nova Scotia to Smith, Dec. 13, 2001.

Chapter 5

[58] "Men of Iron," Dacorum Museum Advisory Committee Information Sheet, 1991, Berkhamsted, England, 1991.

[59] A brassier is a person who works with brass.

[60] Quaker marriage certificate of Joseph Cranstone and Maria Lefevre, D/Ece/F29, Hertfordshire Archives & Local Studies, Hertford, England.

[61] "Men of Iron," Berkhamsted. 1991.

[62] Royal Academy Schools Student Book, (London: Royal Academy of Arts, 1840).

[63] Helen Valentine, ed.*, Art in the Age of Queen Victoria – Treasures from Royal Academy,* (London: Royal Academy of Arts, 1999).

[64] Dacorum Heritage Trust Newsletter, Berkhamsted, England., No. 16, July 1999.

[65] *The Exhibition of the Royal Academy*, exhibit 660, W. Clowes and Sons, London, 1845, p.30.

[66] Johnson, Comp. *Works Exhibited*, exhibit 414, p.111.

[67] *The Exhibition of the Royal Academy,* exhibit 424, W. Clowes and Sons, London, 1850, p.21.

[68] *London City Directory.* London, England. 1847-48.

[69]Cranstone, Family History Notes.

[70] William Powell Frith, *My Autobiography and Reminiscences,* (New York: Harper & Brothers, 1888), V.1.

[71] William Sharp. *Dante Gabriel Rossetti: A Record and a Study,* (New York: AMS Press, 1970).

[72] Sotheby's London, lot 205, sale of Sept. 15, 2000.

[73] Graham Reynolds, *Painters of the Victorian Scene*, (London: B. T. Batsford, 1953) p. 57.

[74] Christopher Wood. *Victorian Panorama: Paintings of Victorian Life,* (London: Faber and Faber, 1976).

[75] 1851 British Census, National Archives, England, HO107/1879/275/57.

[76] *The Exhibition of the Royal Academy,* exhibit 1236, W. Clowes and Sons, London, 1854, p. 45.

[77] Elizabeth Buteux, *Times Highway,* (Berkhamsted, England, Dacorum Heritage Trust Ltd, 1998) p. 68.

[78] Marriage Certificate, No. 34, July 4, 1855, Hemel Hempstead, England, Family Records Center, London, England.

[79] 1851 British Census, National Archives, England, HO107/1715/134/41.

[80] *Ibid*, HO/107/1715/134/27.

[81] Kelly's Directory of Hertfordshire, England for 1866.

[82] 1861 British Census, National Archives, England, RG9/838/20/33.

[83] Johnson, Comp. *Works Exhibited*, exhibit 204, p.111.

[84] Arthur Cranstone to Miss A. M. Lefevre Dec. 1950, D/ECe/F137, Hertfordshire Archives and Local Studies, Hertford, England.

[85] Biddle and Webb Sale, lot 214, Aug. 3, 1973, Birmingham, England.

[86] James Lawson Sale, lot 183, Apr. 23, 2001, Sydney, Australia.

Chapter 6

[87] Cranstone, Family History Notes.

[88] John Cole, *The Clermont Club 1887-1987*, (Clermont, Queensland, Australia: The Foundation Members, 1987), p. 2.

[89] Cranstone Family History Notes.

[90] Captain George Morgan captained the 200 foot long, 35 foot wide 994 ton ship *Ann Duthie* built in Aberdeen, Scotland in 1868; *Lloyd's Registry of British and Foreign Shipping, 1882-83,* Cox and Wyman, Printers, London, 1883.

[91] Crew and Passenger List, *Ann Duthie*, Shipping Master Department, Sydney Harbor, Jan. 18, 1883, Microfilm, National Library of Australia, Canberra, Australia.

[92] *Sydney Morning Herald*, Jan.19, 1883.

[93] Nancy Cranstone, letter, Nov. 27, 1948, D/Ecc/F2/1, Hertfordshire Archives and Local Studies, Hertford, England.

[94] *Peak Downs Telegram*, Clermont, Queensland, Australia, Feb. 23, 1883.

[95] *Ibid*, Apr. 13, 1883.

[96] *Ibid*, June 8, 1887.

[97] *Ibid*, Oct. 21, 1885.

[98] *Rockhampton Morning Bulletin*, Rockhampton, Queensland, Australia, Aug. 29, 1884.

[99] *Ibid*, Aug. 26, 1885.

[100] *Ibid.*

[101] *Rockhampton Morning Bulletin*, Dec. 17, 1889.

[102] Nancy Cranstone, letter, Nov. 27, 1948, Hertfordshire Archives and Local Studies, Hertford, England.

[103] Deutscher Fine Art Sale, Lots 30 and 31, Carlton, Victoria, Australia, Nov. 25 – Dec. 11, 1987.

[104] Christie, Manson & Woods Sale, lots 189 and 190, Melbourne, Victoria, Australia, Mar. 14-15, 1972.

[105] *Peak Downs Telegram*, Feb. 4, 1888.

[106] *Ibid.,* Feb. 18, 1888.

[107] *Ibid.*, Apr. 16, 1889.

[108] *Rockhampton Morning Bulletin*, Dec. 17, 1889.

[109] Death certificate, entry 10132, Sept. 18, 1906, Victorian Records Office, Melbourne, Australia.

[110] Nancy Cranstone, letter, Nov. 27, 1948.

[111] *The Queensland, Australia Post Directory*, 1889.

[112] Death certificate, entry 13490, Jul. 28, 1919, Victorian Records Office, Melbourne, Australia.

[113] Obituary, *Sydney Morning Herald*, Nov. 25, 1988.

[114] *Brisbane City Directory*, Brisbane, Queensland, Australia, 1893.

[115] *Ibid.*

[116] Marriage certificate, no. 1313, May 26, 1897, Brisbane, Colony of Queensland, Australia.

[117] Obituary, *Brisbane Courier*, June 24, 1893.

[118] Death certificate, no. 26096, June 22, 1883, Brisbane, Colony of Queensland, Australia.

BIBLIOGRAPHY

Art Works from the Collection of the John Oxley Library, State Library of Queensland. Brisbane, Queensland, Australia: Library Board of Queensland, 1987.

Bénézit, E. Dictionnaire Critique et Documentaire des Peintres, Sculpteurs, Dessinateurs et Graveurs. Paris: Librairie Gründ, 1976, Vol. III.

Blunt, E. and G. W. Blunt, *American Lloyds, Registry of American and Foreign Shipping.* New York: E. & G. W. Blunt, 1862.

Buley, R. Carlyle. *The Old Northwest: Pioneer Period, 1815-1840.* Indianapolis: Indiana Historical Society, 1950.

Buteux, Elizabeth. *Time's Highway: The High Street, Hemel Hempstead.* Berkhamsted, Hertfordshire, Eng.: Dacorum Heritage Trust, 1998.

Cuthbert, John A. *Early Art and Artists in West Virginia: An Introduction and Biographical Dictionary.* Morgantown, W. Va.: West Virginia University Press, 2000.

Evans, Susanna. *Historic Brisbane and Its Early Artists: A Pictorial History.* Brisbane: Boolarong Publications, 1982.

Fischer, David Hackett and James C. Kelly. *Away, I'm Bound Away: Virginia and the Westward Movement.* Richmond, Va.: Virginia Historical Society, 1993.

Frith, William Powell. *My Autobiography and Reminiscences.* Vol. I. New York: Harper & Brothers, 1888.

Gibson, Langhorne. *Cabell's Canal: The Story of the James River and Kanawha Canal.* Richmond, Va.: Commodore Press, 2000.

Graves, Algernon. *The British Institution, 1806-1867: A Complete Dictionary of Contributors and Their Work.* London: George Bell and Sons, 1908.
_____. *Dictionary of Artists Who Have Exhibited Works in the Principal London Exhibitions from 1760 to 1893.* 3rd ed. with additions and corrections. Bath, Eng.: Kingsmead Reprints, 1901

Reprinted 1970.

Groce, George and David H. Wallace. *The New York Historical Society's Dictionary of Artists in America 1564-1860.* New Haven, Conn.: Yale University Press, 1975.

Harper, J. Russell. *Early Painters and Engravers in Canada.* Toronto: University of Toronto Press, 1970.

Hinshaw, William Wade, ed. *Encyclopedia of American Quaker Genealogy,* Vol. 6, Ann Arbor, Mi., Edward Brothers, Inc., Printers, 1950.

Jackson, Ronald Vern, ed. *Virginia 1860 Federal Census Excluding Present Day Virginia.* North Salt Lake City, Utah: Accelerated Indexing Systems International, 1988, Vol. 1: *A thru K.*

Johnson, Jane, Comp. *Works Exhibited at the Royal Society of British Artists 1824-1893.* Woodbridge, Suffolk, Eng.: Antique Collectors' Club, 1990.

M. & M. Karolik. *Collection of American Water Colors & Drawings, 1800-1875,* Vol. II. Boston: Museum of Fine Arts, 1962,

Kelly, James C., and William M. Rasmussen. *The Virginia Landscape: A Cultural History.* Charlottesville, Virginia.: Howell Press, 2000.

Kloss, William. *Art in the White House: A Nation's Pride.* Washington, D. C.: White House Historical Society, 1992.

Lloyds's Register of British and Foreign Shipping, 1882-1883. London: Cox and Wyman, Printers, 1883.

Maccubbin, Robert P. Ed., *Williamsburg, Virginia: A City Before the State 1699-1999,* Williamsburg, Virginia.: City of Williamsburg, 2000.

Mallalieu, H. L. *The Dictionary of British Watercolour Artists up to 1920.* Woodbridge, Suffolk, England.: Antique Collector's Club, 1986.

Mallett, Daniel Trowbridge. *Mallett's Index of Artists: International-Biographical.* New York: Peter Smith, 1948.

McCulloch, Alan. *The Encyclopedia of Australian Art.* 3rd ed. revised and updated by Susan McCulloch. Honolulu: University of Hawaii Press, 1994.

Money, Maundy, New York Sun, April 29, 1933. Article from London on recent sale of Cranstone's art at London Sotheby's.

Newton, J. H. *History of the Pan-Handle; Historical Collections of the Counties of Ohio, Brooke, Marshall and Hancock, West Virginia.* Wheeling, West Virginia.: J. A. Caldwell, 1879.

Peat, Wilbur D. *Pioneer Painters of Indiana.* Indianapolis: Art Association of Indianapolis, 1954.

Pennington, Estill Curtis. *Look Away: Reality and Sentiment in Southern Art.* Atlanta: Peachtree Publishers, 1989.

Rasmussen, William M. S., and Robert S. Tilton, *Old Virginia: The Pursuit of a Pastoral Ideal.* Charlottesville, Virginia: Howell Press, 2003.

Reynolds, Graham. *Painters of the Victorian Scene.* London: B. T. Batsford, 1953.

Selby, John E. *The Revolution in Virginia: 1775-1783.* Williamsburg, Virginia.: Colonial Williamsburg Foundation, 1988.

Sharp, William. *Dante Gabriel Rossetti, A Record and a Study.* New York: AMS Press, 1970.

Smithsonian Institution Research Information System. http://www.siris.si.edu. Inventories of American Painting and Sculptures, 2002.

"Sold at Auction, water colours by Lefevre James Cranstone at B. F. Stevens and Brown." *Art Weekly*, September 13th, 1928.

"Maxim's Mission". *Time Magazine*, Dec. 28, 1962.

Valentine, Helen, ed. *Art in The Age of Queen Victoria – Treasures from the Royal Academy.* London: Royal Academy of Arts, 1999.

Wood, Christopher. *Victorian Painters.* Dictionary of British Art, Vol. IV,

Woodbridge, Suffolk, England: Antique Collector's Club, 1995.

_____. *Victorian Panorama – Paintings of Victorian Life.*
London: Faber and Faber, 1976, pp. 210-211.

Wright, R. Lewis. *Artists in Virginia before 1900: An Annotated Checklist.*
Charlottesville, Virginia.: University Press of Virginia, Charlottesville,
1983.

INDEX

A

Altmayer, Jay P. 87
Ann Duthie 116, 117

B

B. F. Stevens & Brown Ltd. 4
Bigler, James 55
Bigler's Mill 50, 51, 52, 53, 54, 55, 56, 57, 89, 91, 92, 140
Boston Museum of Fine Arts 95
Bowman, Mrs. Winfred Comstock 4
Bridgeport, Ohio 18, 20, 21, 69, 89
Brisbane General Cemetery 129
Brown, John 63, 64, 88, 131
Buffalo, New York 71, 95, 137

C

Carter, President Jimmy 38, 93
Castle Garden Depot 83
Chandler, J.A.C. 4
Christie, Manson and Woods, London 86, 139, 140, 141
City Stove Store 27
Clermont, Queensland, Australia 116, 120, 122, 123, 125, 126, 138, 145, 146
Cleveland, Ohio 71, 72
Clydebank Cottage 126, 129
Cobh, Ireland 2
Colnaghi, P. & D. & Co., Ltd., London 90, 140
Colonial Williamsburg 5, 90
Comstock, Mr. And Mrs. Paul 4, 37
Cranstone
    Alfred 2, 3, 23, 38, 51, 71, 84, 85, 92, 103
    Arthur 4, 5, 81, 97
    Beatrice Lillia 116, 117, 120, 126, 127, 129
    Edmund 111, 127
    Edward Lefevre 126
    Eleanor Lillia 126
    Frederick 1, 100, 116, 117, 120, 126, 127
    George 51, 98, 100, 103, 112

Joseph 51, 98, 99, 100
Lillia 1, 11, 112, 113, 115, 116, 130
Maria Lefevre 26, 99, 100
Mary 126
Nancy Rose 126
Sarah Pollard 98, 99
Thomas 99, 126
William 1, 3, 26, 27, 37, 51, 100, 116, 120, 125, 126

D

Dacorum Heritage Trust Ltd. 97, 101, 104, 106, 107, 108, 109, 110, 111, 112, 117, 118, 119, 123, 124, 125, 144, 145, 147
Donaldson, Miss E. 111

E

Evergreen Cemetery 81

F

Fort Clinton 83
Fort Henry 11
Frith, William Powell 104, 105, 147
Fugitive Etchings 105

G

Gadebridge Park 100, 101
Goodwin, Rev. William A.R. 4

H

Halifax, Nova Scotia 2, 8, 9, 89, 97, 144
Harper's Ferry 10, 63, 64, 65, 88, 89, 91, 95, 109, 122, 138
Heath Lane Cemetery 115
Hemel Hempstead 1, 3, 11, 51, 85, 87, 98, 99, 100, 101, 102, 105, 106, 111, 112, 113, 114, 115, 116, 130, 140, 141, 143, 145, 147
Hempfield and Wheeling Railroad 12, 16
Henry, Patrick 45, 48
Henry Stevens' Son and Stiles 4
Hill House 113
Huguenots 26, 99

I

Indiana Historical Society 93, 136, 144, 147

Indiana University Foundation 4, 5
Innes, Georgiana 113

J

James River 45, 46, 47, 50, 92, 140, 143, 147
Jeffrey, Capt. James M. 2
Jenings, Edmund 51, 54
John Oxley Library, Brisbane Australia 111, 120, 121, 127, 128, 147

K

Kangaroo 1, 2, 8, 9, 10
Karolik, Maxim 95, 137, 148
Kent, Miss Ellen 116
Kentish, William 10

L

Lefevre
        Albert 26, 27
        Gertrude 26
        Ellen 26, 27, 126
        Frederick 26, 27
        Maria 99
        Sarah 99
        Thomas 99, 126
        William M., Jr. 27
Lewis, Wilmar 93
Lilly Library 4, 6, 7, 8, 9, 10, 12, 13, 14, 15, 16, 17, 18, 19, 20, 21, 22, 23,
        24, 25, 26, 28, 29, 30, 31, 32, 33, 34, 35, 36, 37, 38, 39, 40, 41, 42,
        43, 44, 45, 46, 47, 48, 49, 50, 51, 52, 53, 54, 55, 56, 57, 58, 59, 60,
        61, 62, 63, 64, 65, 66, 67, 68, 69, 70, 71, 72, 73, 74, 75, 76, 77, 78,
        79, 80, 81, 82, 83, 84, 88, 89, 137, 142
Liverpool 1, 2, 7, 85
Longford Monthly Meeting of Friends 99

M

McCulloch, Samuel 11
McCulloch's Leap 11, 12, 16, 17
Mellon, Paul 91, 92, 137
Messenger
        Ann 112
        Annie 112

Lillia 112, 113, 130
Thomas 112
Murray, John, Earl of Dunmore 58

N

Nainly, Hannah 51
Newberry, William 111
New York 1, 2, 7, 9, 10, 26, 51, 55, 71, 81, 83, 90, 95, 96, 132, 136
Niagara Falls 74, 77, 81, 89
Niagara River 79, 140

O

Oglebay Institute Mansion Museum 95, 96, 136

P

Parkersburg, West Virginia 10, 23, 25, 26, 89, 136
Partridge, Asa 11, 38
Peak Downs Hospital 116, 120, 122, 138
Philbrick
Elizabeth Ann 11
Joseph 11
Pollard, Sarah 98, 99
Porto Bello 58

Q

Queenstown, Ireland 2, 7, 84

R

Randolph, Peyton 58
Richmond, Indiana 1, 3, 4, 10, 25, 26, 27, 28, 29, 30, 31, 32, 33, 34, 35, 36, 37, 89, 93, 95, 96, 113, 136, 137, 140, 142, 143, 144
Richmond, Virginia 45, 46, 47, 48, 49, 85, 86, 87, 89, 91, 134, 137, 140, 143, 144
Richmond Art Museum 37, 96, 113, 137
Ripon Hall 51, 54, 55, 89, 92
Robinson, T.R. 89, 97, 139
Rockefeller,
John D., Jr. 4, 89
John D., IV 94
Rockhampton, Queensland, Australia 120, 138
Rockhampton School of Arts 120, 122, 138

Rollins, Mrs. J. 26
Rossetti. Dante Gabriel 104, 145, 149
Royal Academy of Art 42, 101
Royal Society of British Artists 86, 103, 137, 138
Rugg, Martha K. 76
Runnels
     Lilley T. 11
     Mary 11
     Nancy B. 11
     Washington 11

S

Sass, Henry, School of Art 101, 104
Shockoe Bottom 86
Smythe, Rebecca 26
Sotheby and Co., London 86, 89, 91, 97, 139, 140
St. Mary's Church 101, 102, 107
Sterling and Francine Clark Art Institute 97
Symonds, Winifred Nellie 126

T

Toowang Cemetery, Brisbane, Australia 129
Turnor
     Edmund 127
     Edmunda Lillia 127
     Graham Augustus 127

U

Utica, New York 26, 81

V

Vigo 83, 84, 85, 143
Virginia Historical Society 86, 87, 91, 137, 140
Virginia House 91
Virginia Museum of Fine Arts 92, 144

W

Washington, D.C. 41, 64, 89, 93, 143
Weddell, Alexander W. 91, 144
West Point, Virginia 50, 51
Wheeling, West Virginia 3, 10, 89, 91, 94, 95, 96, 136, 142

Wheeling Creek 11, 12, 14, 67, 68, 95, 97
Whitewater River 33
White House, The 38, 93
"White House" 113, 114, 116
Williamsburg, Virginia 3, 4, 5, 50, 51, 52, 53, 54, 55, 58, 59, 60, 61, 62,
     63, 89, 90, 103, 142, 143, 144, 148, 149
Woods, Colonel Arthur 5, 90